T0072296

ATHENA

A Goddess has returned

Marcus Mcnally

BALBOA.PRESS

A DIVISION OF HAY HOUSE

Balboa Press books may be ordered through booksellers or by contacting:

Balboa Press
A Division of Hay House
1663 Liberty Drive
Bloomington, IN 47403
www.balboapress.com
844-682-1282

Because of the dynamic nature of the Internet, any web addresses or links contained in this book may have changed since publication and may no longer be valid. The views expressed in this work are solely those of the author and do not necessarily reflect the views of the publisher, and the publisher hereby disclaims any responsibility for them.

The author of this book does not dispense medical advice or prescribe the use of any technique as a form of treatment for physical, emotional, or medical problems without the advice of a physician, either directly or indirectly. The intent of the author is only to offer information of a general nature to help you in your quest for emotional and spiritual well-being. In the event you use any of the information in this book for yourself, which is your constitutional right, the author and the publisher assume no responsibility for your actions.

This book is a work of non-fiction. Unless otherwise noted, the author and the publisher make no explicit guarantees as to the accuracy of the information contained in this book and in some cases, names of people and places have been altered to protect their privacy.

Any people depicted in stock imagery provided by Getty Images are models, and such images are being used for illustrative purposes only. Certain stock imagery © Getty Images.

Print information available on the last page.

ISBN: 979-8-7652-2777-0 (sc)
ISBN: 979-8-7652-2778-7 (e)

Balboa Press rev. date: 04/29/2022

This is a reclamation of your virginity, before heaven.

Mocking a female deity is grounds for divorce.

There is not one hint of inequality, between woman, man, that is a lie, a handed down lie, a suppression device keeping the woman's soul under influence.

CONTENTS

ABOUT THE BOOK

Athena is a small look into a lifetime's fill of spiritual seeking. It is a complicated mix of the emotional struggle in finding relief from this world. The story is an odd tale to Ithaca and Ithaca has not arrived. The profession of a Goddess returned who longs to live in the heart of those she loves. The reclamation of your virginity, before heaven. No man stands between you and your Goddess. Live and the let live but love one another. My views are progressive otherwise I might be deemed a hypocrite. Athena is a hard stance on the side of nature, nature is unequaled intelligence. My digs at science are aimed at its blindness, just like religion, it cannot see outside of itself, locked into the human mind, a creation of earth. If you are blind to the hosts, the hosts are blind to you.

As for the writing of Athena I believed it necessary, to keep the statements said at the time of writing, unaltered as much as possible to keep my post thought ego out of the way of the original energy, poor spelling, poor grammar, erratic tones, expressive words, ideals and gestures, keeping the energy of real-life experience, present throughout the book. My apologies to all those that I have offended, by the writing of this book. Athena reins supreme

Sincerely
Marcus 4/28/2022

About the author,
I am a spiritual seeker who found his god.

THE EVENT

First Published Nov 2017, event took place July 2017.

I f one ever reads enlightened spiritual text, this event is not completely unique, some details are of course unique to me, but context and events following lead to the same self-realization, and this is the story. After almost 5 years my interpretation of the story has changed, but this is what I was thinking and being told. As this last year unfolded, there came the Mary revelations, gnostic revelations, women, world peace, and lastly Athena.

Weeks prior to this event, was the conclusion of some very tumultuous years of ups and downs, Alcoholic Anonymous, rehabs, counseling, the Army, bible doctrine and yoga, this last one was different. I started in on yoga and participated in a teacher training, but the intentions became for my awakening, I wanted to see. I felt it in my heart and knew that I was not seeing all there was.

Shawnee, Oklahoma Original story Nov 2017

I was at the Holiday Inn express, Rm 427 I'm thinking the whole place is haunted not just 1 but 100's All shapes and sizes, some doing stuff some waiting for something. When I came into the room I knew I had been there before I was sure. Then everything started coming back to me I was in a state of complete peace as I was supposed to be here. The general manager is why I was sent, I was sent to raise her energy, the ghosts asked the universe for help, the lady or general manager is some sort of caretaker of the ghosts, but she is in complete disbelief. I had seen the lady in a dream twice differing in age of about 10 yrs but that was her. I told her I was here to help. So, to make a story short I asked her and she stated there are no ghost. I told her it was abuse for her to not acknowledge them, especially her. I was fired from my job and asked to leave the hotel. After that I saw ghosts everywhere, I mean everywhere. Its like they are saying thanks or yes we do exists and are looking for a way to communicate. I mean they were everywhere, I never experienced something like that. I went to another hotel and that's when they started coming around, I allowed to come close I welcomed them trust me it was stand up on your hair but not terror just like someone you know sneaking up on you. Since then my energy has changed a bit, but as expressed my story, doubt, fear and disbelief and anger has been thrown my way. I have some pictures and a video. I am big believer in the universe and the oneness of all things, there is no fear because they are part of this universe just as much as I am. I have never been into paranormal stuff, I am kind still not. But this is my story and its real. From this experience I can tell you shapes sizes, energy feel and they are wanting to communicate, there is a lot more.

That story is no dream, and apparently I been promoted to some sort of medium maybe I don't know I see and feel spirits, Its get dark after that I was afraid to sleep with lights off, but that subsided, but what this did do was push me into deeper into meditation practice, I was slightly awake before now, what took blasted away blocks. I am a devotee to the Hua Hu Ching, with that said here is what is taking place now.

I had this deep sense of knowing that I have never not existed, and then a couple hours later walking into Walmart, an overwhelming, epiphany came over me, that said I am consciousness, the same consciousness that is in everything around us, I walked in Walmart in a daze made it my back to my car, and started texting a friend, as I look up a dragon fly is hoovering outside my car window staring at me, I was filled with complete joy, went home laid down for a couple hours in state of peace and joy. I have moments with lizards, birds and overwhelming desire to save the world, water has on taken a whole new meaning. Last night I had cock roach on my counter, It made its way on to my hand, and let me put it outside, it was a very surreal moment, lol. I can do harm not intentionally to plants, people, beings, even dark entities can be forgiven.

Right before all this took place I went though some of the deepest pain, ego love attachment, but soul contracts come and go. I had relapsed on drugs, came out of it got back into my yoga practice and then relapsed again then went through this whole scenario. What I think I know, I had went through before and I didn't make it, I made it this time, the 427 room was some sort of other dimension, a recording a replay of some script, because half through, I dawned me I already did this, and started remembering like a movie I saw. This is no hallucination, if I did not have pictures, I would be in a lot of trouble externally and internally. I was in a state of severe doubt because of the drug use days prior but the universe saw me and knew. This whole experience has taught me to quit doubting just because some else and especially myself has not experienced or doesn't believe. The layers to this lesson can be applied to every aspect of human endeavors. Doubt and fear are limiting inferior ways of thought a walking prison conditioned by other walking prisoners to afraid to step outside and see there is no prison at all.

Thanks
Marcus

I removed the names, dates, and location, so not to injure my myself or others further with unwanted solicitation, doubt or skepticism.

THE WHITE PIGEON

E vents and thoughts are written down in present moment experience, April 2021 thru Sept 2021 very little added or taken from original transcript, but the experience remains real.

April 2021

So, earlier this week I was watching Accession Keepers, Ep 10 The Carthars and the Lady of Light. I was thinking to myself, how come I have not seen this white dove or pigeon. Maybe two days later, this white pigeon shows up, on a telephone wire, I drive right under it. There is astonishment to what I am seeing. What I am supposed to say to that, no that did not happen? I emailed William Henry, I told the story, the story as follows.

whenrytn@earthlink.netTue, Apr 6, 2021 at 5:13 AM

Dear Henry

The message is believe in humanity. That is our salvation. This will confront the image, I cannot predict the future, but I do know, that image is a lie and must be confronted. If the message becomes about anything other than humanity, the message will be lost, and will be taken over by the image. Meaning no one personality can lead the charge. Love has no doctrine. Why believe me? Believe the message and understand its depth. It came from heaven. My son 19 recently had the kundalini/holy spirit event, he is marked to learn to Sanskrit, obsessed with it. I spent 2 to 3 days in the spirit world, I was told I was sent to raise the vibrational frequency of the planet. July 2017 9-11 It was a full moon. I did not understand the message, I do now. The message is not about me, it fails if becomes about me, even a hint, humans love to worship the image, the image is on a path to destroy us. Unity is what is needed, without the personality. It is an original message. I have large gongs facing one another in my living room with some odd sacred geometry on my wall, that I did not methodically put there, it just showed up. I have tasted heaven with the gongs some spirit takes over and produces some explicable joy a taste of heaven. I morphed into some fanatical state, but I cannot and will not do it alone. Its not my job, it our job to believe in humanity, humanity is you. I had also, what could be the spirit of God come on me, that said that "fire is coming from above, love is the fire that is coming, change your ways". It also told whatever has this planet under deception to get the "FUCK THE OUT"! That was the language, very direct. Anyway, that is the message. I hope this finds ears of understanding.

Sincerely
Marcus

"Believe in Humanity." That same week, at lunch thinking about emailing about the white pigeon, it flies by twice. So, I email him again, a little less cryptic, there is no cryptic about it, its a truth. Email follows

<u>*whenrytn@earthlink.net*</u> *Wed, Apr 7, 2021 at 12:47 PM*

I have been watching your documentary series ascension keepers. A day after that episode, a large white pigeon has appeared, even at lunch today l am thinking about emailing you and this I assume it to be the same bird flys by twice. I believe in the message. 100% there is no returning back to back to the image I have made my stand. Believe in Humanity! It will give us our power, which is wasted away into the false image. The bible has some curse on it. I was a hard thumping Christian for many years. Gnosis is the way, love is the way.

I am not selling myself; I am trying to get you to buy in to believing in one another. Two days after I come for lunch in my spot, I am late. There is a mockingbird waiting on the barb wire. Within a minute the mockingbird was gone, and the white pigeon flew and landed on some branches. I was able to get pictures. Email follows

To:whenrytn@earthlink.net Fri, Apr 9, 2021 at 12:52 PM
The picture of the white pigeon was the content of the email.

It is not the Lady of Light, it's a white pigeon passing on a message. 3 times I saw the white pigeon, maybe I see it again, but 3 times and I am telling the story I am figuring things out as I go, there is deep significance, to what is taking place. I must tell the story, I love the story, it's about us. Believe in one another.

The 4th time was on the way home in highway traffic, the white pigeon dashed in front of my car and circled around then kept pace for about 2-3 or seconds, that night I posted the original story on Facebook.

5th The white pigeon showed up again today. 6/4/2021, I saw a white bird, I thought it was an egret. I sat in my car, eating a snack. As I got out, it flew by very fast, then circled around and slowed down. I was able to draw energy from her today, Mary, I take it. Peace and that is what I felt, peace.

6th was my rear-view mirror at lunch a few days before the 7th

7/2/2021 The white pigeon appeared on phone wire outside of work, that was 7th appearance. I wonder if that will, be it?

7/23/21

9/15/21 I saw the white pigeon today with my son, the message was about Satan. Before I changed my tune about the nature of angels good and bad.

There was a hint of doubt that passed through my mind about the white pigeon, and its connection to the shadow or the lie, it was immediately blasted away, like a ball of power pushing out.

The path is shown, it's not up for debate. There is no backing down, I believe the message, believe in one another. This is our course correction, it could only come from a no-one, like a seed that has been planted, it the energy will flourish, that is the given path. No matter what comes of it, this is a proclamation, "Believe in Humanity, Humanity is YOU". Discovery what this means The information is already out there, change the way you view the information.

I thought then that I might have taken on the soul of Mary, the white pigeon was the carrier that day in the exchange, they have been waiting for me to evolve, or someone or be receptive or the empty enough. I have had countless transmissions seen and felt spirits come and go. It dawned on me what has taken place and then it never occurred 4 years ago in the hotel that this was going to be what it is, I still don't know. As for Mary and the soul, those are up for debate, I just know that something has taking place related to this. Old thoughts

Real life events create the fanatics, if Jesus did not believe in what sent him, he would not have died on a cross, he would have continued to build houses and die of natural causes

I am an empty vessel.

Shortly after that I ordered the Gnostic Bible, read the gospel of Mary. then the proclamation "Believe in Humanity is you" "Mary of Magdala has come for the women of the world" A present female deity. that is what I am passing on.

the white pigeon

THE BOOK
OF NAAS

O ATH OF SACRED If you would know what eye has not seen nor ear heard and what has not arisen in the human heart, and who stands high above all good, swear to keep the mystery of instruction sacred. The mother, who saw the good perfected in her, has kept the mysteries of silence sacred. She has sworn and will not waver. Here is her oath: "I swear by the one overall, which is the Good, to keep these mysteries, sacred and tell them to everyone, and to go from the Good back to the creation."

When you take this oath, you enter the Good and see what eye has not seen nor ear heard and what has not arisen in the human heart. You drink from the living water, the washing, the spring of living water bubbling up. And there was a separation of waters from waters, and the waters below the firmament belong to creation. In them are washed those who are earthly and psychical. The waters above the firmament belong to the Good and are alive. The spiritual and the living are washed in them as Edem was after the washing. She did not waver.

THE SAGA OF THE CREATORS There were three ungenerated principles governing the cosmos: one Unknown, one male and one female. The Unknown principle is called the Good, and it alone carries that epithet and knows everything ahead of time. The female principle is named mother of all things begotten in the world, and she is known and visible. The male is angry. He knows nothing ahead of time and he has two minds and two bodies, he is a child above and a viper below. He is called both Elohim and Israel. These are the principles of the cosmos, the roots and pools from which all sprang, and nothing else was in the world.

When the father knowing nothing beforehand saw the virgin Edem, he burned for her, and he the father is called Elohim, and Edem for Elohim. Their love drew them to a single union. From this union the father seeded twelve angels for himself. The paternal angels are Michael, Amen, Baruch, Gabriel, Esaddaeus, Metatron, Azzael, Uzza, Azza, Rapheal, Uriel, and Lucifer

Edem seeded maternal angels to govern creation, Babel,

Achamoth, Naas, Bel, Belias, Satan, Sael, Adonaios, Kauithan, Pharaoth, Karkamenos, and Lathen. Of these twenty-four the paternal ones sided with the father and obey his will in everything, and the maternal ones hear their mothers voice, Edem. Their common domain is paradise, about which Miriam tells us,

"God planted paradise east of Eden, before the face of Edem, and therefore she always looks at paradise, her angels. The angels of paradise are allegorically called trees, and the tree of life is the third maternal angel, and her name is Naas, while the tree of the knowledge of good and evil is the third paternal angel, and he is Baruch. Miriam spoke these things covertly because not everyone can hold the truth.

THE CREATION OF ADAM AND EVE After paradise came into being through the love of Edem, the angels took some of the best earth from that good earth they made woman, also from the good earth came wild beasts and creatures. They made woman a symbol of their union and love and planted some of their powers in her. Edem provided the soul and Elohim the spirit. The woman Eve was a seal and memory of their love, an eternal symbol of the wedding of Edem and Elohim. And, as Miriam wrote, Eve was image and symbol, and the seal of Edem preserved forever. Edem set the soul in Eve and Elohim the spirit.

And they were given commandments: "Be fruitful and multiply and live in peace with the earth. Edem gave away all her power to Elohim, like a marriage dowry of yesteryear, in imitation of that first marriage, a woman comes to her husband with a dowry, obeying a holy and hereditary law that Edem carried out toward Elohim.

THE ANGELS ARE DIVIDED When, according to Miriam, everything was created including heaven and earth and all therein, the twelve angels of the father were divided into four principles, and each quadrant is called a river: Pishon, Gihon, Tigris, and Euphrates. Huddled in these four parts, the twelve angels circle around and govern the cosmos. Their authority over the world comes from Elohim. They are not forever in the same region, but as in a circular chorus they move from place to place at fixed intervals and periods according to their assignments. When the angels of Pishon rule a region, then famine, distress, and tribulation foul that segment of the earth, for their criterion for ruling is avarice. And in all regions come bad times and disease according to each power and nature. There is a torrent of evil pouring out like the rivers, and constantly around the world Elohim's will controls every quadrant.

Edem's ASCENT The consequence of evil has this circumstance: when Elohim and Edem made the cosmos, Edem chose to rise to the highest part of heaven to see if their creation lacked any elements. She took her angels with her and rose, as was her nature, and she left Elohim below, who being bound to passions of creation declined to follow Edem upward. When Edem reached the upper border of heaven, she saw a light stronger than the sun she created, and she said, "Open the gates for me to enter and to acknowledge the lord. I had thought I was the lord!" She heard a voice out of the light, saying, "This is the lord's gate. The just pass through it. The gate was immediately opened, and the mother, with her angels, went into the Good and saw what eye has not seen or ear heard and what has not arisen in the human heart. The Good said to her, "Sit down at my right hand. The mother said to the Good, "Let me restore in the cosmos I made. My soul is imprisoned among people. I want to take it back. Then the Good told her, "Nothing which comes from me can be evil. In your love you and Elohim made the world. Let Elohim keep the world as long as he wishes, but you must stay with me."

Elohim's RESPONSE Then Elohim knew he was rejected by Edem and angerly began to gather angels around him and adorn himself brightly to arouse her return. But under the Good's control Edem no longer descended to Elohim. Then Elohim commanded Lucifer, to incite fornication and divorce among people, so that as he was separated from Edem the soul of Elohim in people might feel affliction and be tormented and suffer like him, Elohim, her rejected co-creator. And Elohim gave grand authority to Baruch, his third angel, to torture the soul of Edem in people with all possible tortures so through that spirit Edem might herself be tortured—she who had dissolved her covenant with Elohim in just cause.

EDEM SENDS DOWN HER ANGEL NAAS When the mother Edem saw these things, she sent down Naas, her own third angel, to comfort the spirit living in all people. When Naas came, she stood among the angels of Elohim, in the midst of paradise. Paradise was the angels among whom she stood, and she commanded the people "to eat from every tree in paradise, except from the tree of the knowledge of good and evil," which tree is Baruch. They could obey the other eleven angels of Elohim, for though they have passions they do not disobey the commandment. But Baruch disobeyed. He approached Eve and seduced her and debauched her, which is a transgression, and he approached Adam and played with him as a boy, which is a transgression. So, adultery and pederasty were born. Since then, evil and good have ruled people. It began from a single source. When the mother ascended to the Good, she showed the way for those who wish to rise, and by leaving Elohim she began to take back her soul in people.

NAAS SEARCHES FOR A SAVIOR Naas went to Miriam and spoke through Moses to the children of Israel to turn them back to the Good, but Elohim's third angel Baruch barred her way. Through the spirit Elohim gave her and Moses and all people, Baruch expunged Naas's orders and only Baruch's commandments were heard, and so spirit was set against soul. The soul is Edem while the spirit is Elohim, and each is in both man and woman.

Then Naas was sent down to the prophets so that the soul living in people might hear and flee from Elohim's corruption once Edem disavowed their covenant. But Baruch, using his old tactics, dragged the mother's soul down into the spirit of people he seduced, who scorned Naas's words in Edem's commandments. Then Naas chose a prophet from the uncircumcised, Herakles, and sent him to subdue the twelve angels of Elohim, and free the mother's soul from the twelve evil angels of the Elohim. These are the twelve labors in which Herakles contended, from first to last, with the lion, the hydra, the boar, and the rest. And they are names of nations given to them from the power of the paternal angels. Just when he seemed victorious, Rapheal attacked him and took away his strength and Naas's commandments ordered by Edem, and then he wrapped him in his own robe, the power of Elohim, the power from below. Herakles' prophecies and work were nothing.

NAAS FINDS JESUS Finally, "in the days of king Herod, Naas was sent once more by Edem and she came to Nazareth and found Jesus, son of Joseph and Mary, feeding sheep, a boy of twelve and she told him everything that had happened from the beginning, from Edem and Elohim and all that will be. She said, "All the prophets before you were seduced, but Jesus, earthly son, try not to be seduced, and preach the word to people and tell them about the mother and the Good, and ascend to the Good and sit with Edem, mother of us all."

JESUS' CRUCIFIXION AND ASCENT And Jesus obeyed the angel. He said, "Lord, I will do all things." He affirmed this. Baruch wanted to seduce him too, but he could not. Jesus kept faith with Naas. Then Baruch was enraged because he could not seduce him and he had him crucified. Jesus left his body to Edem by the tree and ascended to the Good. He said to her, "Woman, here is your son. He left his spirit and earthly body, but his soul he placed in the hands of the mother and then he ascended to the Good.

Then Miriam the prophetess, the sister of Aaron, took a tambourine in her hand, and all the women went out after her with tambourines and dancing. And Miriam sang to them: "Sing to the LORD, for she has triumphed gloriously; the horse and his rider he has thrown into the sea."

Revised and restored to more correctly fit Justin's original story.
by Marcus

Reference the book of Baruch by Justin

Chapter 1

ATHENA

Self-worth is everything

T he stars shined upon earth with love that only heaven could
understand.
Athena throws her javelin, Mary in stride on the wings of heaven
Believe in you, believe in humanity
The Birds
Believe in humanity, humanity is you
Athena gives her the confidence deep in her heart,
Athena gives him the confidence deep in his heart,
The gods give us the confidence deep in our hearts,
the goddess who presides in human meetings

Mother Goddess, hear my prayer
Without the mother there is no father, without the father there
is no mother. Is one greater than the other? The orphan child has
neither father nor mother to call their own. The orphan child
only see's the father, the mother is not understood. Who took this
understanding away? Does the orphaned daughter, submit to the
orphaned son, if the mother is understood? Mother Goddess, hear
my prayer and help me understand. The orphaned daughter is in the
care of the Mother Goddess, no longer the victim of the blind Father,
who does not hear the prayers of his orphaned children. The choice
remains in the hands of the children, and whether they wish to be
orphans any longer. The once Bright-eyed child of Zeus has become
the Mother Goddess, and longs to be the adoptive Mother of the
orphaned children. The Mother believes in the children. Hearing is
the Mother the children hear her voice. The blind and deaf father
remains blind and deaf, in the leftover memories of printed text.
Let go of the printed text of the blind father and find the Mother
Goddess. I Believe in the Mother and the Father, the choice remains
with you. It is the mother who takes care of the children, why
has she been oppressed by the blind father? The stars shine down
upon earth with a love that only heaven understands. Without Yin

there is no Yang, Mother Goddess hear my prayer. Believe in the Goddess, the Goddess puts forth only love, therefore the Goddess in return receives love, because that is all the Goddess has is love. If we believe the Goddess, I want to know the love of the Goddess. Does the current God understand love? Or does he only understand fear? What say you? What does the man say? Or is the man afraid to speak? This is the overthrow of the vengeful God, what say you? The Goddess grew up and has chosen the path of love. The Goddess came by the way of the dark path and has chosen what it is better. The Goddess speaks for you. The Goddess lives in the heart

It matters not what the man says, what does the woman say?

Thousands of years later, the woman still is not free. The life of the woman is still crippled by the restraints of segregation and the chains of discrimination, that come from religious ignorance that has robbed her of god power, Thousands of years later the woman lives on a lonely island of fear amid a vast ocean of god equality. Thousands of years later, the woman is still languished in the corners of the worlds societies and finds herself an exile in her own land. And so, we've come here today to dramatize a shameful condition.

Martin Luther King, Jr.

The wars of yesteryear have been reduced to a pounding on the wall and a single engine plane flying overhead No longer do the fields of artillery remain, from the shelter from the bombs overhead

The father has a daughter
Judgement follows
The dead have spoken
The popes stand condemned
With great joy and great sadness, the death of popes
In a vision of an old man dressed in white, not the Pope, but another
The Catholic Church

Blind does not describe, blind is forgivable, the institution of the Pope and that government will not be forgiven.

You are the problem you sell god for money, and you are conscious of your lie

Your ways are not my ways

Does the church deserve judgment from deception? That remains in the churches

The Church of Christ is ignorant of its possession of the soul and heaven, heaven does not discriminate. Finding a Revelations scripture to fit the meaning, is a of waste time on ignorance, not the scripture, just the ignorance.

The International Churches of Christ is just a branch of the government that stems from the Vatican, Vatican rule remains locked in the bible.

"Your desire shall be contrary to your husband, but he shall rule over you"

What a horrible curse to be lived and believed, what a gross ignorant deity, who gives this deity power? Christianity does, by believing in the bible you keep the curse alive. Shame, thousands of years later it remains alive and locked in the most printed book ever.

I say again: If anyone is preaching to you a gospel contrary to the one you received, let him be accursed.

Did Jesus teach that?

The history of mankind is a history of repeated injuries and usurpation on the part of man and God scripture toward woman, having in direct object the establishment of an absolute tyranny over her.
Elizabeth Cady Stanton
God scripture add on
Athena

Jesus said to him, "I am l the way, and the truth, and the life. No one comes to the Father except through me.

5

He prepared us and made us truly human."
And he said Whoever discovers what these sayings mean will not taste death.

What I teach, is the way the truth and the life, not my death on a cross.

Then Mary stood up,

Church doctrine about the inequality of man to woman is a disgrace, it is a direct insult in the face of god, in the face of creation.

The way of Confucius is rank and title, the way of heaven is freedom.

Mentors, people we esteem more than our selves. My mentor growing was not true, my likes were not in line with the one I esteemed. Nobody cares, the birds care, I fight for the birds. This is about us, you cannot oppress women, physically, mentally, spiritually, it is against the laws of nature. These religions are in violation of heaven. Porn is in violation of heaven. The Americana woman says we are not oppressed; your vagina is powerless. Deceit is no way to live, the perception that men worship the vagina is false, once the seed is spilled you are worthless. Porn is the constant spilling of seeds on the ground, followed by disgust from the man's heart, towards the woman. Because you are not worthy of God in their eyes, it remains acceptable in the heart of man to oppress, the one that esteems him. Not all men, that would be in insult on creation. The religious man who professed his divinity then judges his sisters as something unequal to himself. Your ways are not way my ways, your ways are the problem.

Lao Tzu

The teenage boy is irresponsible with his penis. Porn is a weapon that should not be handled by boys or even adults, who are not responsible with their penis. Porn should not be handled at all it is a deadly poison that sits on the soul

The spirit speaks, the woman has not spoken
We do not know, what the woman's point of view is.

Paul had messed up beliefs, he did not see the whole story, he passed those beliefs on to us unknowingly. We inherited his dysfunction, then other distortions factor in as well, to what was passed on to us, over the course of 2000 yrs. The ignorance to claiming his doctrine to absolute truth, is beyond stupidity, there is no excuse for that ignorance.

I did not leave you without faith only a change in perception

Your repentance is confirmation
The Birds

Pressing a movement on the authority of a female godhead, Athena. This changes our world.

The freedom of the bird becomes conscious in the heart.

This is the written notice of the return, Athena a goddess. Your ways are not my ways.

If your beliefs in your deities do not bring you to world peace then what good are your deities, that leave you only in conflict with your sister.

If we establish churches of Athena, we reestablish, the woman's authority, a belief in the birds, a belief in nature. A belief in Humanity. That is the goal.

I believe in Athena. I have my faith. I look up at the stars, we look through a pee hole into the universe, and think we know it all. There are a trillion earths, and something fights to hold on to possession of ours. My stomach is still upset, The guru describes, but he doesn't know the way. And only for price, will he give you the time of day.

Athena is a super solider deity; her government speaks below. Freedom never comes without sacrifice

The movement is based on the woman's roles with family, the core family is the foundation of society. At the core of the woman is this incredible integrity, we are looking to restore this core of integrity to our planet. The career is secondary to family, what is the woman's point of view.

I believe in Athena
I want to know this goddess
Athena is within, Athena is a goddess head

The statue of Liberty is a woman, the statue of the idea liberty is a woman.
Athena

Women have always fought for a man's truth, but could not see that her truth was just as important
Abess Yin

There are not bad people there are just bad governments
The Nymphs

Buddhist is a label, just like Christian, don't get lost in the label
Abess Yin and Mary

The Dalai Lama is in error of Buddhism
Abess Yin

During a moment of expression of gratitude, the conclusion and felt truth is, that we the whole planet is ruled under spiritual tyranny
Abess Yin

It matters not, it matters not what the other person does.
Abess Yin

The nature of consciousness is in front of your face.

Faith is meant to be more than some obscure phenomena

You are on the verge of destruction, because you think you know, a gross disgusting ignorance sits over us, Blind, Blind, Blind!!

We accept human cruelty as some ignorant evolutionary process we grow out of, pushing the blame to nature. Yet the man with all the knowledge of the evolution is blind to nature and consciousness.

A religious awakening, Athena is within, not the western image, but the eastern deity of the One true self. This is nature, the sun, the moon, clouds, the birds, insects, animals, fish and rivers, oceans, life, with a goddess head. A goddess has returned. I am her witness; Believe in Athena.

Athena is a goddess head, a god head for women and men alike releasing women and men from bondage of the male deity, that says she is second to man.

You are judged for the look of your skin, hiding behind adornments, the self-worth remains with the adornment.

We become holy women and holy men, nothing stands between you and your god.

We are let back into the garden of Eden

We find god in the new age, and we write new scripture

Athena

We come together under one banner and form a government and we preach equality. A spiritual government, one that encompasses the whole of the earth. I grew up fearing Islam, does Islam provide anything more than fear?

The Birds, woman's best friend, the freedom of the bird becomes conscious in the heart.

Green peace, give Green Peace authority, they are the zealots, not the profiteers, therefor they can be trusted with earth's assets.

We need to believe in the demons, if you do not believe in the demons, you cannot see the demons, demons are stupid, that is the energy they carry, stupidity. Let us join our minds together and build a weapon that can kill us all.

The earth is a non-discriminant being that produces to feed its populations, the earth is danger of dying from exhaustion.

The earth fund, we were all in darkness at one time.
The Dolphin

Athena could have told Telemachus, that Odysseus was alive, but instead the goddess with blazing eyes, gave him the courage to make his own stand. The wisdom of the gods.
The Great Egret, spiritual experience precedes commentary, if there no experience how can there be commentary?

Defining Religious Crazy
The mind is impaired the gods speak
We impair the mind for wickedness and accept its cause, but when we impair the mind to speak with the gods we call it lunacy
You could have 15 and 15 living side by side those that desire the Brahmin. The Hua Hu Ching
We look at the world differently by drinking Soma. Agni.
Giving credit to the gods, after a saying or quote, I certainly cannot take credit for it, I could but where did it come from? To the Brahmin priest a sweet drink is Soma, a delightful drink a gods favor. The Buddha speaks a grand thought and then the subtle speaks, who else am I going to give credit to? Everyone speaks, everyone gets the credit. The gods speak to those in favor of the gods, become in favor of the gods and let go of the searching in dated scripture, and have the gods speak to you. Once a glorious task, but if all can hear what the gods are saying what need is the glory in speaking with the gods. Let the Brahmin priestess drink Soma and hear what the

Goddess is saying. The pressing of Soma is the pressing of the soul, wine is a release. The priestess and the birds, what are birds saying to the priestess who drinks Soma? The Brahmin priest calls on the Brahim priestess to press Soma and express the soul. It reminds us of life and death. Abess Yin. Pressing Soma is the expression of the soul. Abess Yin. The Brahmin priest is not Soma. The priestess does not where a white robe to be a priestess. The Hua Hu Ching. Why would a Brahmin priestess reject its wisdom? Yeshua. If I am not hear for the awakening of the planet, then why am I here? Krishna. We look at the world differently by the drinking of Soma. Agni. If your desire is the Brahmin, sex will not let you pass. The Solar gods. The Brahmin priest speaks. Marcus.

I also had an angel appear in a dream, an angel with blazing eyes, Athena's trademark look. Dec 2020, my understanding knowledge of Athena has come only this last week December 2021, announced by a statue in my room of two Nymphs, that said, We believe, then, Athena, a goddess has returned. The message comes with unyielding convictions on human and nature's rights.

I had a white pigeon appear after asking for it, over a period of 3 months. It landed on this, Athena, the message must be true. This is about faith!

It comes down to worship, not knowledge

Stronger United
Then Mary stood up
and two red roses

Chapter 2

THE WOMAN'S RIGHTS

Self-worth is everything

I am the voice of the women who are unable to speak." "They think this is a man's country, but it is not, it is a woman's country too." *Farhat Popalzai,*

I looked through an office window yesterday and saw a computer screen with a desktop display featuring two beautiful flowers, women are beautiful, just like the flowers.

When, in the course of human events, it becomes necessary for one portion of the family of man to assume among the people of the earth a position different from that which they have hitherto occupied, but one to which the laws of nature and of nature's God entitle them, a decent respect to the opinions of mankind requires that they should declare the causes that impel them to such a course.

We hold these truths to be self-evident: that all men and women are created equal; that they are endowed by their Creator with certain inalienable rights; that among these are life, liberty, and the pursuit of happiness; that to secure these rights governments are instituted, deriving their powers from the Consent of the governed Whenever any form of government becomes destructive of these rights, it is the right of those who suffer from it to refuse allegiance to it, and to insist upon the institution of a new government, laying its foundation on such principles, and organizing its powers in such form, as to them shall seem most likely to effect their safety and happiness.

Prudence, indeed, will dictate that governments long established should not be changed for light and transient causes; and accordingly all experience hath shown that mankind are more disposed to suffer, while evils are sufferable, than to right themselves by abolishing the forms to which they are accustomed, but when a long train of abuses and usurpations, pursuing invariably the same object, evinces a design to reduce them under absolute despotism, it is their duty to throw off such government, and to provide new guards for their future security. Such has been the patient sufferance of women under this government, and such is now the necessity which constrains them to demand the equal station to which they are entitled.

The woman thought to win her equality was to compete with the man, through the man's lens, not understanding she was already equal, she needed to see through her own lens and not the lens' of the man. Women are afraid of men, because they see through the created fear of the man's lens. Men create conflict in fear of each other, pushing the blame to language, nationality, religion, ideology, wrongdoing, but won't admit it is fear. Better to fight then admit fear, the acceptance of fear brings peace and understanding. Voice it out loud that you are afraid of men. Feel the fear in you heart and let it go. This gives you power over the fear.

It is a small world, if one is oppressed then all are oppressed. If you are still persuaded men are your superior, voting for men to press your rights, but those men do not press women's rights, what difference does your vote make. Equal population, low women's numbers in office. You are not a voice, just a follower. Persuaded by the man to vote one way or another, not by the woman. How can you be woman if man is telling you what to do? Do not accept partial equality from that something that would have never given you equality, in heart or mind.

The burqa is a symptom of extreme fear coming from the Muslim male. There is no breaking free of this fear in Islam

Islam, Christianity, Judaism, all have the same father.

Athena is the female archetype of the new age, mocking a female deity is grounds for divorce.

The statue of liberty is a woman

Whatever laws binding you to religious inequality you are released.

It matters not what the man says, what does the woman say?

The vision is a separate government worldwide or women are in complete control of the planet, a switching of roles. No longer held hostage by the male ego.

Porn is attached to the worst people on the planet, sex traffickers, rapist, pedophiles, murders and the like, they care nothing for the well-being of their fellow human or the planet, demons in human skin. Our government allows this to flow freely through our airwaves, unchecked in the hands of every person with a cell phone. We call this freedom of speech

The Nymphs

We don't want a government; we just want to be free

The Nymphs

The nymphomaniac what freedom is there in its existence

The Nymphs

People want purpose, the preacher worries about collections, unconcerned about purpose. The seeker seeks, the preacher seeks collections

The Nymphs

Tell me your thoughts. It is demonic what is inside our heads. Violent thoughts lead to violent actions. The news projects violent actions.

The Nymphs

A girl when she is young never says to herself, I want to sell my body for money.

The Nymphs

It is 100% belief in emotional equality and judgment equality; the scripture is the problem. It plugs into the higher mind, the god mind, and says it is not equal. Seeing the amount of doubt in our world, the religion lies, if our source to god is a lie, the mind knows no truth, and creates from doubt, competition for truth, not food, it is unending, Men believing that they are unequaled on earth, creates unbalance and because they are the perceived top dog, will not hear anything other than, a revolution is the only course to bring balance. We have been seriously out of balance for a long time, men have rejected women, as judgment equals, the man rejected emotion, condemning it to weakness, not wisdom. By rejecting emotion, he rejects half of himself and cannot see or hear. Women have fought tooth and nail to claim rightful status, that fight has not ended and to stop short of complete equality on all counts for the entire world, is destruction for all. A slows miserable death, where men of no morality or integrity hold billions hostage only for a display of power. Government is about resource management, not power.

(66) Yeshua said, Show me the stone that the builders rejected. That is the cornerstone.

Is the woman's way better than the man's way? Our world is running the man's way.

There is not one hint of inequality, that exists between a man and woman. That is a lie, that is a handed down lie. A suppression device keeping the woman's soul under influence.

The vision is a separate government worldwide or women are in complete control of the planet, a switching of roles. No longer held hostage by the male ego.

Why are old men, still creating laws about women and their bodies? What is the problem?

The Gospel of Mary

The Woman's Bible

The unbalanced masculine principle is failing this planet. *"The stone the builders rejected has become the corner stone, The Lord has done this and it is marvelous in our eyes."*

The male leadership of this planet has been nothing but disastrous, the man has insisted with blood, that this world is ran his way, his way has failed. His way only produces more fear.

You remove man and the God deity, what is the full protentional of women.

For so far-reaching and momentous a reform as her complete independence, an entire revolution in all existing institutions is inevitable.

Reformers who are always compromising, have not yet grasped the idea that truth is the only safe ground to stand upon.

for all the religions on the face of the earth degrade her, and so long as woman accepts the position that they assign her, her emancipation is impossible.

Though familiar with "the designs of God," trained in Biblical research and higher criticism, interpreters of signs and symbols and Egyptian hieroglyphics, learned astronomers and astrologers, yet they cannot twist out of the Old or New Testaments a message of justice, liberty or equality from God to the women of the nineteenth century!
21ˢᵗ Century

Oh, mighty preacher of the word of God, where has your power gone? Maybe Peter or Paul can give you some advice from their extensive knowledge of a woman's place in society
Yeshua

Firmly relying upon the final triumph of the Right and the True, we do this day affix our signatures to this declaration.

Susan B Anthony, What does it matter what I look like, I am beautiful. Having to add her name, a transmission came through that communicated, she was speaking from heaven. She has new a body that is beautiful, just like the one she had on earth, except there is no judgment, to say any different than beautiful.

Lucretia Mott
Margaret Pryor
Elizabeth Cady Stanton
Eunice Newton Foote
Mary Ann M'Clintock
Margaret Schooley
Martha C. Wright
Jane C. Hunt
Amy Post
Catharine F. Stebbins
Mary Ann Frink
Lydia Mount
Delia Mathews
Catharine C. Paine

Elizabeth W. M'Clintock
Malvina Seymour
Phebe Mosher
Catharine Shaw
Deborah Scott
Sarah Hallowell
Mary M'Clintock
Mary Gilbert
Sophrone Taylor
Cynthia Davis
Hannah Plant
Lucy Jones
Sarah Whitney
Mary H. Hallowell
Elizabeth Conklin
Sally Pitcher
Mary Conklin
Susan Quinn
Mary S. Mirror
Phebe King
Julia Ann Drake
Charlotte Woodward
Martha Underhill
Dorothy Mathews
Eunice Barker
Sarah R. Woods
Lydia Gild
Sarah Hoffman
Elizabeth Leslie
Martha Ridley
Rachel D. Bonnel
Betsey Tewksbury
Rhoda Palmer
Margaret Jenkins

Cynthia Fuller
Mary Martin
P. A. Culvert
Susan R. Doty
Rebecca Race
Sarah A. Mosher
Mary E. Vail
Lucy Spalding
Lavinia Latham
Sarah Smith
Eliza Martin
Maria E. Wilbur
Elizabeth D. Smith
Caroline Barker
Ann Porter
Experience Gibbs
Antoinette E. Segur
Hannah J. Latham
Sarah Sisson

If a man speaks or acts with an impure mind, suffering follows him as the wheel of the cart follows the Beast that draws it
The Buddha

He has withheld from her rights which are given to the most ignorant and degraded men - both natives and foreigners.

He has compelled her to submit to laws, in the formation of which she had no voice.

The woman is for the most part always in submission to the man, modern terms. Sex, Dress, food, entertainment, religion. Laws are stereotypes, which control behavior through fear.

Google is the highway into hell, countless porn sites with a single word referring to the female anatomy. If think you are not oppressed, then you are deceived.

He has never permitted her to exercise her inalienable right to the elective franchise.

Let go of the ways of the male ego and no longer listen to it voice, the possession of its eyes, the desires of the genitals and the lies of conquest, instead of generosity

The priests abused the children, entrusted to them by the mothers. The trust of the woman violated by the name of God.

Women, Self-worth is everything

Take my spirit and go be woman

This was preceded by a well of emotion, that pressed out of my heart, thousands of years under unjust rule, man but know not woman.

Women are now and the future; they are an untapped resource

Women have tremendous power to guide this planet into a different direction, one of peace compassion, generosity and stability.

No dude is better than you

I boycotted Amazon for the most part kindle is a library owned by amazon it is hard to separate, is it hypocrisy on my part. Without Amazon I would not have access to material, but at the sometime that is the way oppression works. June 2021 or sometime before it matters not.

I boycotted Amazon because of the penis its trademarked company emblem, it is a penis. If you have doubts, look at his rocket ship. The Amazon smile is a penis in your face.

There are these open wounds that exists within the human sphere, the wounds bleed, until we acknowledge them, they will continue to tear us apart. They exist on the subtle level; the wounds remain open in the world's religions.

In politics the creation of a Women's party, unyielding

There is this idea that there has to be some uprising, but to continue in the lie of God, that you are second to a man, ever!

The male deity of yoga, the image of those that brought yoga posture to the west does not fill the bucket nor can it. Only you can fill the bucket, that image is a lie Those images abuse their power.

The energy shared between men and women is distorted. The man feels one thing and woman feels another, but both are felt in the body.

Fear is a psychic energy, that communicates without words

The job of antidepressants and a counselor is to get off counseling, and the antidepressant, not be fed to another and given another drug.

We are being shown two sources of confidence in Mary's enlightenment, each coming from each other, there is also the before and after death experiences, this is confidence. From Jesus to Mary, Mary to Jesus.

If someone else has already had the honor of recognizing, Mary as an Apostle, then I second that for eternity. If it is of great privilege to recognize her and her contribution to humanity. She became and showed us what it meant to be human. Let her take her seat in the great of greats that has transcended our world.

How I view women and why I believe the way I do. For the first thing, to me I do not understand this view of something less than, ever, so seeing it is easy. Even during my heavy biblical days, I thought of the lunacy behind the thought, but I did not understand its significance. Women have been oppressed for millennia; it is just the way things are. There was no real resistance to the oppression, after a while, things changed women started speaking up, they had a voice but did not really have a real say into the way things are. This lack of power created an energy of doubt, some energy that lacked confidence, so even though women are the equal, just the other side of the coin, that inequality said one half of the coin is inferior. So, this lack of confidence lends itself to a debilitating expenditure of energy trying to please, and gain confidence from the male opposite, which is unconscious and primarily ego, and does not have the confidence to give, due to its competitive nature. As, I emerged from my own oppressed self, I did not understand why women lacked this ability to love openly, without reservation. This image of love that women portrayed this deep feminine divinity, is buried in doubt and fear. It is not free, the man always wants to control or get something from the woman.

The path out is a difficult road to follow, there is just absolutely so much hate in the world. Love is taught, and this world doesn't teach it. It teaches competition instead of collaboration. This ongoing competition for nothing has scarred our world. The roots stem from an oppressive creator that blamed the feminine for the grief that plagues humanity, that is a heavy burden. The oppressive creator is a lie. This weight upon the psyche has lessened due to the awakening of the divine feminine, but its roots remain in the world religions.

Letting go

Chapter 3

THE BIRDS

Self-worth is everything
The Birds

The birds bring deep understanding of the spirit. Their speech is of the higher mind, that is the voice of the universal mind, that is the voice of god. There is no doubt to this statement. The birds represent more than just synchronicities with nature. I can't say enough about the birds, a living present intelligence, that builds faith with interactions. All of nature is alive and aware.

I saw this incredible bird on a wire before your yoga today, I thought to myself, my heart yearned to be closer to this being. I want to know its creator. It was a king fisher

The students said to Yeshua, Tell us what the kingdom of heaven is like. He said to them, It is like a mustard seed, the tiniest of seeds, but when it falls on prepared soil, it produces a great plant and becomes a shelter for the birds of heaven.

The bird carries in her heart Speech that the divine youth spoke of inside the womb. The poets guard this revelation that shines like the sun in the footprint of Order.

If there is one chapter to this story that carry's the most weight it must be this one, the Birds. What I have right now not is enough to describe the intelligence of the kingdom of the birds. The gods show themselves to those in favor of the gods. One story, the crows, the white pigeon, the grackles, but the whole story is about us. The birds are simply trying to remind us of who we are, a part of creation of nature. A piece of the earth loved and adored by the gods. That is a message of the birds. Some stories are meant for another time, in a book I will read from someone else's experience with the birds. We kill children in the womb, yet broadcast cast nature as cruel and ignorant if the birds don't have all their offspring survive the nest. If we broadcast the cruelty, we put children through, maybe we would see our own ignorance, and not view our ourselves as superior, just because we can broadcast.

Lesson number 1 Society has a choice, one is the apple, and the other is a Ding Dong, society is sick and has many diseases, if we chose the apple, all goes well, if we continue to choose the Ding Dong, society remains sick and has many diseases and is danger of not recovering.

If science preached a healthy lifestyle and prescribed this as medication, instead of the chemical substitute, what becomes of the Ding Dongs. What cure does Science have for the Ding Dong? We trust our health care providers to give us the right advice, these are our trusted physicians, will that be a diet or regular coke, sir? Next please.

Science has no cure for the Ding Dong

The Nymphs

Lesson number 2 the gods do not see garbage they see what we need.

The male driven society bent on conquest, instead of generosity Jesus came to seek and save what was lost.

What gross a feeling that is one pounding on the wall and the other desires peace. The birds sing the walls they pound.

The gods are always working to improve themselves for us, perfection is not understood.

We need the Elephants for our survival, we need wildlife for our survival.

It is raining the weather sucks, discrimination toward nature

The mother duck unknowing leads her family into danger, humans being the danger, the human says stupid duck, the discrimination of the mind toward nature.

It is not the bird's job to conform to us, but us to understand the birds

I believe in the birds

You come into this state of trust, that says I don't know, but the energy of trust leads the way. Trust is the energy.

The bird sitting on top of a cage is symbolic of freedom. At least in my book it is.

Can this be real? Does nature really communicate in such ways? Science says nature is blind, the sun rises and the sun sets, one sun and one moon.

Once again, I will try to expound on the birds, if one word does it, conscious, nature is not blind, we are blind and deaf.

The great egret, spiritual experience precedes commentary, if there no experience how can there be commentary? For me the realizations come out of nowhere, two pictures in the bathroom, one of a great egret and the other, a family of herons. The great egret came first, the spiritual experience came second, the realization came last.

The egret on the car, in a tree off in the distance are some white birds, I wonder what type of birds those are, about an hour later I go out to the car, and a great egret is on the hood of another car a few feet away, welcome to the Egrets. The cattle egret was the culprit or maybe it was the Ibis, but the birds made their introduction.

A lunch time meditation and a flash of red, a cattle egret appears, a few hours later looking through a bay door a narrow vantage point and a cattle egret appears, the spirit came first.

Walking into a supermarket, a sparrow flies at a car door as if trying to get in, in the supermarket a man with flowers for someone at church, that man owned the car, the birds knew beforehand about this connection. The sparrow came first, the man second and the realization last.

In math you cannot explain the equation If you didn't work the problem, the universe has its laws, why are spiritual laws any different? As I drive to a supermarket unknown to me my head is in a fury, the cattle egret swoops by, my head and body are relieved of its fury. An hour later haphazardly sitting on my porch, a cattle egret strolls by a moment too soon or late, the connection is not understood. I text a friend, out of the joy of the moment.

On the freeway drives, I begin to wonder have the egrets been here the whole time. Do they migrate? Or have I just been blind? A feather for the birds, and a collection of north America, the collection came first, the feather came second, the realization came last. 123 the sacred order.

I asked the Crows for a feather, I was given a whole bird, there was this explosion of joy over the matter, then the doubt was thrust into my mind. Is it really a crow or is it a grackle? The instruction begins, I have trouble with the beaks, the grackles start appearing beaks raised high to see the silhouette, that doubt continues, my mind will not let me believe it is a crow. It is in my freezer I examine it again, again and again, I see the tufted of hair on the beak, the blackness of the feathers and the energy screams crow, but my mind will not let go of the doubt. The grackles it seems are mocking my ignorance, what value do I give to the grackles? Are the crows more important, why does it have to be a crow in the freezer won't any bird do? The doubt continues, later that week, I drive into a supermarket, I see two dead crows, I go get them, a sacrifice to quell my doubt. I email the Crow Nations of the experience, out of my joy, and yet the doubt lingered for months. In the end I buried the crows and gave the spirit back, the crows come around and visit. My doubt was finally quenched, but not without help from the birds, that is what they do, wildlife is other intelligent life we destroy with no conscious.

The birds are this incredible, synchronistic living being all around us, it not just the birds. My view at work, a giant blue sun rising and another at midday. The sun rising seen through a window, a bay door with a view for the birds. Seeing how they live and interact, this incredible array of life in between two buildings on pavement. Pinecones from trees it goes on, and two women feeding

I go to a Publix this morning, I see an incredible bird, they are all incredible, but a little more so at first glance. I go in, I come out, I see the bird once again, it flies to a wire. At home the sunlight shines on a bird that fits the description. Right in the heart of the Sunbird, on the North American collection, a common myna

My own faith is questioned by these events, is this true?

Fifty crows, Saturday full moon before sunset, something says go outside I sit outside 50 crows fly overhead. In interaction with the crows these last few months, there is no doubt there is hierarchy. Not seen but watched in movement. Coming and going on command. Being in one place, then a minute later, not one to be seen. A mass of crows swoops down and land in formation on a power line.

The story throughout is glittered with inspirations from the birds, The birds, they are a daily journal

An email sent to the EPA, copied to Green Peace

I was walking in this large field by my home, 50 birds fly around this cell tower, then they all go land on a high antenna, the old type. I walk over to the cell tower, warnings posted about the dangers, and FCC regulations. Who protects the birds? I emailed the EPA do I need data? To prove this harm to the birds do you need to kill to collect data?

Science tortures and kills nature to get its information, they view themselves as intelligent because they can remember how to spell but cannot remember that they are life as well.

It began with the egrets or maybe it was the crows or maybe the sparrows, the jays, the seagulls or maybe it was the pigeons, who at one time I killed in ignorance or a black bird I shot with a bb gun, believing that was a superior way. Killing what is innocent for the sake of praise of or attention or accomplishment The birds bring deep understanding of the spirit. Their speech is of the higher mind, that is the voice of the universal mind, that is the voice of god. Animals in general see the un appended subtle body.

Just now crows coming back from Walmart, I drive into my apartment complex, 3 crows sitting on the dumpster, a caw, and then a flurry of crows fly by as I drive in. I just believe, that is what that is, a letting go of doubt. This relationship that produces gratitude for living.

The experience with birds, not captive, not forced, looked for yes and no, but the birds are something else we have not come to understand, under the same oppression as the divine feminine. It is language spoken and understood by the spirit. There is great sadness at this realization because of great ignorance coming from our lack of understanding, brought about by our spiritual oppression. The birds are something special, someone says I am looking to become someone and instead of looking for change, a judgment of motive

The sparrows, cardinals, hummingbirds, black birds, ducks, mockingbirds, jays, hawks, pigeons, swallow's, the eagles, the egrets, the doves, the dragon flies, the bees, insects, spiders, trees and bushes and list will go on, it is unrecognized life that is all around all the time. It is the breath to the body, without the breath there is no life.

Yesterday I was sitting quietly, and a crow and songbird where discussing something it was meant for me, I was given approval of some sort, a trust. That is the connection to beauty and life that is all around us. The oppression of the holy spirit, If Christians knew that the holy spirit is mother nature, what would the world look like. The holy spirit is the mother.

There is always a discrimination coming towards nature from the mind, the mind believes it is superior to nature

The discrimination against beauty, the preference of one to the other. Even at its most delicate state.

The shadow on the wall, the connection with nature, faith is built upon from what we gather around us. It becomes real in an unreal world.

I did a sound bath tonight, I was little agitated, not feeling well. I come home clear and prepped for a gift from the birds

Just now I have been feeling a discrimination towards the birds, that they were less than. I went to type this pushing past the discrimination, I heard the crow caw, in my head or outside I do not know. I felt an immediate clearing of that energy.

Artificial intelligence, is at war with life, artificial doesn't mean science fiction

The proper use of meditation, spiritual practice and psychedelics, the birds understand their function. there is a profoundly deep connection to everything. Instead, of being at war with nature, there is harmony. The harmony is what the monotheistic, one God image does not want you to see or understand. It is the image that blinds us. There is this dance with life that we do not see.

Last night 10-28-21 I was sitting quietly a voice says you are about to be promoted, I felt joy, didn't know what to think. Looked over at the at Sunflower, and the Sunflower says, you are the son of man. I immediately felt this rush of peace and joy. I did not know what to think, but just had to believe. That peace sits on me right now. Joy that is what I feel. Responsibility.

The totems from the birds. The totems are lines of communication into the subtle mind. They reveal what the mind is thinking, bring it to forefront so the thought can be recognized.

A totem received THE BIRD PECKED SEEDS OUT OF THE SUNFLOWER.

To the uniformed this is spiritual practice which is worship. Cannabis is a bridge

The beauty is recognized, with understanding from the bridge this carries over into daily life.

The bird pecked seeds out of the sunflower, as I typed I felt another discrimination toward Susan B Anthony let go. I discriminated her religious views.

The bird pecked seeds of discrimination out of the sunflower don't take a picture of me, understanding both sides the bird pecked seeds from the sunflower

Discrimination against the famous, the bird pecked seeds of discrimination out of the sunflower

That is our problem, it is a spiritual malady of the way we look and judge one another that is what it means. They are pearls from heaven, do not give your pearls to the pigs

Bird speech
When they set in motion the first beginning of speech, giving names, their most pure and perfectly guarded secret was revealed through love.

When the wise ones fashioned speech with their thought, sifting it as grain is sifted through a sieve, then friends recognized their friendships. A good sign was placed on their speech.

I love worship

Chapter 4

CHIEF BLACK HAWK

Self-worth is everything

The native Americans deserve a star and a stripe on the American flag, 2 seats in the senate and 10 seats in house of representatives. And electoral votes of any of the biggest states. Make your opinion count and take back your power. It is your country too.

Chief Black Hawk

I did not know who Chief Black Hawk was until two days ago in a meditation gong ritual, at the end of the gongs, an energy rushed through me, and Chief Black Hawk came into my mind, this is the inspiration for this chapter, and it started with asking the Crows for a feather and in return I received 3 birds leaving no doubt about the message. All events are expressed in present moment experience. The birds were returned to the earth, and their spirits back to the Crows.

Surrender Speech

Black hawk is an Indian. He has done nothing for which an Indian ought to be ashamed. He has fought for his countrymen, the squaws and papooses, against white men, who came, year after year, to cheat them and take away their lands. You know the cause of our making war. It is known to all white men. They ought to be ashamed of it. The white men despise the Indians and drive them from their homes. But the Indians are not deceitful. The white men speak bad of the Indian, and look at him spitefully. But the Indian does not tell lies; Indians do not steal.

An Indian, who is as bad as the white men, could not live in our nation; he would be put to death, and eat up by the wolves. The white men are bad schoolmasters; they carry false looks, and deal in false actions; they smile in the face of the poor Indian to cheat him; they shake them by the hand to gain their confidence, to make them drunk, to deceive them, and ruin our wives. We told them to let us alone, and keep away from us; but they followed on, and beset our paths, and they coiled themselves among us, like the snake. They poisoned us by their touch. We were not safe. We lived in danger. We were becoming like them, hypocrites and liars, adulterers, lazy drones, all talkers, and no workers.

We looked up to the Great Spirit. We went to our great father. We were encouraged. His great council gave us fair words and big promises; but we got no satisfaction. Things were growing worse. There were no deer in the forest. The opossum and beaver were fled; the springs were drying up, and our squaws and papooses without victuals to keep them from starving; we called a great council, and built a large fire. The spirit of our fathers arose and spoke to us to avenge our wrongs or die. We all spoke before the council fire. It was warm and pleasant. We set up the war-whoop, and dug up the tomahawk; our knives were ready, and the heart of Black-hawk swelled high in his bosom, when he led his warriors to battle. He is satisfied. He will go to the world of spirits contented. He has done his duty. His father will meet him there, and commend him.

The earth listens to those she trusts, the earthquakes, storms, the calling of the bison at the command of the gods was because earth trusted the deities. The gods went different directions and the trust of the earth was lost to conflict, some gods became angry and went to war with the earth. Their power is all but gone lost to the image, nothing remains of their former greatness, just a lie concealing their identity.

The bible replaced that which was superior, with something inferior. It might not have replaced it in your heart, but it made itself better than what you believed in, calling you less than. What you knew beyond doubt was true, the bible claims it to be false. Not only does it claim itself superior, it forces you to claim it also. Faith is a fine line, I learned faith through the bible, but I had no other. If the bible was true, it would have reestablished your prior freedom. But it pages have only brought sorrow. The caw of the crow, crickets, the tweets of sparrows, the fluttering of doves, the odd stare of the egrets, screeching hawks, the grackles, the jays, cardinals, ducks, mockingbird, pigeons, eagles, lizards, roaches, ants, bees, spiders, dragon flies', rabbits and squirrels, frogs, animals, trees and bushes, lakes and rivers, sun, moon, stars, planets, clouds, winds and rain. heat and cold, the smell of beauty in short, the beauty of life, has no sorrow.

The Natives, the outside looking in, what happen? I might not know what it is like to be native, but as I came into my knowledge of god, I realized the native had something the white man never touched or understood, and this is harmony with creation, the native could have lived millions of years, and not know that a million years has passed. As for his counterpart, a few hundred years and we are scraping the bottom of the bowl, hoping that we can make it last, until we come to our senses. And we call this civilized society, from natures point of view, civilized society is destruction. Better to remain uncivilized and live a million years, than allowing the chains of civilization, wipe you from the face of creation. The savage, what a compliment! The Braves! The Warriors! The Black Hawks! The Indians! The Red Skins! The Tribes, these long admired images of courage and strength, tuned into mascots, not for us to ridicule but as a reminder for the native of your created greatness, that did not need a label, but lived in the heart, true greatness, a creation of god. So, when a university, bears your name, it is not an insult or persecution, a grand gesture from heaven to native, remember who you are. The spirit speaks in such ways.

My ways, were your ways
Athena

Chief Black Hawk
The white demon has never told the truth, its mission has been always to consume and control, the fight has never been in the physical realm, it is not flesh and blood but in the spirit realm where the real fight takes place, control the mind, control the spirit. Masks on our children setting up next the generation for complete submission, even for those who saw through the lie, but did not stand up to the lie, the imprinting on the psyche of the child remains, needles and bottles instead of a healthy free life, the mind buried in a screen, that speaks lies.

The vision of the demon, an ethereal shape shifter, a thousand faces with every name. Doubt and fear it knows no other, attaching to sources to keep it from annihilation. Continually shifting its face in fear of discovery, upon discovery doubt is thrust back, due to the doubt that it, the demon, exist at all. It dwells in doubt and fear it cannot see any light, a voice in the head an energy in the body. Unconscious it comes and goes as it pleases, mindful and the fight begins. The birds see and the birds hear, nature sees, and nature hears. A constant reminder of plain truth, fighting against manufactured truth.

The spirit of the fathers saw the demons, and did not see the physical, the fight has always been in the ethereal realm. They spoke, they talked, this is real, the demons are real. Live free or die, spiritually. That is what the fathers meant. There was no right or wrong just a demon sitting on the soul. The Indian in the past before the settlers, understood and was closer to god than the bible believing Christian. There is a score to settle with demons. The bible does not recognize creation, therefor the Christian does not recognize god, you must see to be seen.

"A Poem by Tecumseh "So live your life that the fear of death can never enter your heart. Trouble no one about their religion; respect others in their view, and demand that they respect yours. Love your life, perfect your life, beautify all things in your life. Seek to make your life long and its purpose in the service of your people. Prepare a noble death song for the day when you go over the great divide. Always give a word or a sign of salute when meeting or passing a friend, even a stranger, when in a lonely place. Show respect to all people and grovel to none. When you arise in the morning give thanks for the food and for the joy of living. If you see no reason for giving thanks, the fault lies only in yourself. Abuse no one and no thing, for abuse turns the wise ones to fools and robs the spirit of its vision. When it comes your time to die, be not like those whose hearts are filled with the fear of death, so that when their time comes they weep and pray for a little more time to live their lives over again in a different way. Sing your death song and die like a hero going home."
~ Chief Tecumseh" — ~ Chief Tecumseh

The government outlaws gambling, give it to the reservations, they can have it. The government is morally superior to the Indians. Who does the gambling, the Indians?

Without knowing the feeling of oppression there is no way to break free from it. If you have never been oppressed then you do not know what it is, therefore, you cannot see it. It is in the seeing that enables you to break free of it. These women's rights leaders were white and affluent, the spirit speaks without discrimination of name and form, for all of us.

If you never tackle fear in your own heart for extended periods of time, you can never see where the fear is coming from. Once you address the fears in your own heart, you begin to see that you are not creating the fear, but the fears are being created not from within, but from external influence. An unseen energy a vibration, a frequency, a language, a mechanism.

If a government establishes control over Google, who has your information? Google is witness and a highway to the most destructive evils in the world and does nothing. Yet claims itself as virtuous.

Google is biggest theft of identity in the world. No identity no rights.

In only seeing the physical being, the energy is impenetrable, fear is created because the obstacle is a like rock fortress, if you see the being of subtle matter, then you become equals.

It is about the human heart. The media divides and say it is impossible for change because they broadcast the demon seeds. The media is 100% full of shit, their truth is distorted

We hold these truths to be self-evident: that all men and women are created equal

Elizabeth Cady Stanton

For many of our white brothers and sisters as evidenced by their presence here today, have come to realize that their destiny is tied up with our destiny. And they have come to realize that their freedom is inextricably bound to our freedom.

Martin Luther King, Jr.

The white men are bad schoolmasters; they carry false looks, and deal in false actions.

Chief Black Hawk

Does the gay woman or man believe their rights are more deserving than the woman or the native?

The African American is still languished in the corners of American society and finds himself an exile in his own land

The American Indian is still languished in the corners of American society and finds himself an exile in his own land

The spirit speaks, the native has not spoken

For when the gods have a good fire, they bring us what we wish for. Let us pray with a good fire.

They killed off the bison, now the wolf is a pest to their cattle.

It was trust, the energy of nature is trust. The energy of life is trust. The false image sells security

Each species has a god or goddess attached to it, each with different potencies, when a species goes extinct, the spirit goes with it, just not extinct.

Where did all the Marlin go?

The Dolphin

We need the ozone for survival

If these green supermarkets are so green remove the bags, help the consumer make the right choice

If I am appointed to special role by the ruler, what freedom do I have, If my values far exceed the values of my ruler?

To see the world's problems, you have to separate yourself from the world.

Yeshua said, Look, the sower went out, took a handful of seeds, and scattered them. Some fell on the road and the birds came and pecked them up. Others fell on rock and they did not take root in the soil and did not produce heads of grain. Others fell on thorns and they choked the seeds and worms devoured them. And others fell on good soil and it brought forth a good crop, yielding sixty per measure and one hundred twenty per measure.

For the Christian community, Santa Clause is our first supernatural being, before Jesus. Santa Clause is a god, that turns out to be a lie.

The rulers of the air, they cause our dysfunction

To those that consider themselves to be shamans, can you see the fight?

So, if you look for truth in a book that does not tell the truth, where are you to go? A map giving you the wrong directions.

Through the silence of the mind, nature speaks in an audible voice heard in the language we speak, it is universal.

Our power comes from creation, creation it is all around us, never hiding its face or refusing to give us comfort

When the demon of sunlight pierced you, Sun, with darkness, then all creatures looked like a confused man who does not know where he is.

The Rig Veda demonstrates this harmony with nature, there is no other vehicle in which the hymns come from. This understanding and connection to life, not myth, life. There you always find truth, nature cannot lie, because it is nature, it is god. There you will find peace, power, and prosperity. The pressing of Soma

Our thoughts bring us to diverse callings, setting people apart: the carpenter seeks what is broken, the physician a fracture, and the Brahmin priest seeks one who presses Soma. O drop of Soma, flow for Indra.

Yeshua said, A person old in days will not hesitate to ask a little child seven days old about the place of life, and the person will live.

As you, Indra, struck down the sunlight-demon's magic spells that were turning beneath the sky, then Atri with the fourth incantation found the sun that had been hidden by the darkness pitted against the sacred order.

Press for your rights on how this country is run, reclaim your power, find that truth that governs all. Unity is your power. Integrity is your fortress The bible is not your story. The bible is not about you. You never needed the bible, to maintain a righteous peaceful way of life. You were in harmony with god, getting back to harmony is just a shift in perception, have great fires and call on the Mother Goddess where your ancestors reside.

Nature, Women, Natives, all have oppression coming from the physical and spiritual, who is this oppressor? The masks are like the burqa or head coverings for females, it is a physical restraint of the spiritual body. The scripture tells you one thing, and then delivers another. It is in the spiritual realms that the oppression is taking place. Scripture being the news, the news has become god, telling us what to do, where to go and how to behave. Like the bible it only divides those who watch and believe what it says. It sources like the bible are unchecked and left in the hands of stupid demons. Demons are stupid, that cannot create so they steal and consume.

Removing government and religious oppression, what is the potential for Indians? Do you stay oppressed like a man who does not want to leave prison because he had been there too long?

The animals have no ego, they are who they say they are. Everything pushes into our boundaries something is trying to control us. Always multiple forms of oppression, no one seeks your freedom, because they do not have freedom themselves. Only the freed slave can free slaves. We are slaves to demons. How can earth not be hades, one man holds wealth beyond measure, yet there are those who go without water, yet the one feed from those without water. Bottom feeders, that is what they teach, feed off those that can't feed themselves, Bill Gates and the like.

An ongoing war for freedom, it has nothing to do with the United States but everything to do with us.

Demons are stupid, that is the energy they deserve do not give them any more than, "they are stupid". Their energy only destroys, spiritual warfare. Ignorance being claimed as genius, stupidity. Not people the demon, demons use people as mediums. But this is because they are stupid.

The opossum and beaver were fled; the springs were drying up, and our squaws and papooses without victuals to keep them from starving;

44

we called a great council and built a large fire. The spirit of our fathers arose and spoke to us to avenge our wrongs or die.

Spiritual practice will transform the Native American population back to its true self. This one belief in nature, being called back to god. Greatness and smallness are only a perspective.

A cockroach on my counter, something said leave the cockroach alone, it went into the sink, it paused, I stared, it looked up, we met eyes. Small white, I felt its being, I meditated into its being, it slowly fell asleep. I could I feel its being, the transferring of energy was peace. It stayed asleep for about 15 minutes; I just went to check it is gone. I have residual peace left over in my being, or a remembered connection. It was trust, the energy of nature is trust. The energy of life is trust.

All we can do, therefore, is show the way to the traveler; we cannot walk it for him. We can write the prescription, but we cannot drink the bitter herbal tea for him. All teachings are like medicine which is given to the sick according to the disease they have.

Lao Tzu

Chief Black Hawk

Chapter 5

MARY

Self-worth is everything

I t has become intense I am waiting to get checked, see what happens. It is either real or not real. If it is not real, then what? I guess nothing will happen. It is real we are ruled by demons, who are at the end of their time. Salvation what is that? What does that really mean.

Give up your life for humanity. How does that work? Start fighting for it. It is just a change in perception. It is a spiritual change, it must be. Quit fighting against who we are and embrace change for peace and prosperity, let go of what divides us and bring us together.

That is the kind of commitment it will take to change. It is this complete sell out for humanity, while not neglecting the very thing that supports us, earth. It is in the heart, that says my life is ransom, Jesus says, lose *your life and save it*

Go make disciples, find gnosis and change the world, The fields are ripe for the harvest

The bible does not stand up for women.

Women's rights.

Do not allow the belief in a deity subject you to discrimination. Athena

When we claim belief in a deity, we own that claim, your faith establishes your right to that claim

Self-worth is everything

If you insist on finding your self-worth in a man, it will always be with the man, and not with you.

If a man decides his worth is decided by a women's love his love will always remain with another, and not in himself.

The power of oppression through god discrimination, that god discrimination is a lie. Men in any religion past or present do not own the rights of women, what they deem came from god is a lie.

From birth the Christian way, steals the daughter of the human child.

From birth the woman is convinced, that she will never be good enough to stand equal with god and men.

It is not just the Christian way that does this.

If your religion does not meet your spiritual needs, then do not submit to its authority.

Women's issues should never be decided by a man, unless that man gives the power to the woman.

There are a lot of religious teachings in the world, with thousands of PhD scholars, who claim to know what it was and what it was like to live as the faith makers did. But what they are really doing is trampling god underfoot, lessening the spirit to a place below the intellect putting experience of the moment, into a solution. It is highly doubtful that the intention to do so was evil, but just ignorance. If we come into a knowledge of the truth, do we continue in our ignorance, or do we change? Faith is a prerequisite for heaven, if we don't understand faith, then how can we claim to know what the faith makers know.

The problem with Christianity is you worship a book; you think the whole truth of god is found in a book. You don't understand the life that is all around all the time. You go to church, sing some songs, give some money, and believe that is enough. neglect creation in exchange for judgment of your sister.

We all know there is something missing in our faith, but the fear is that if I deny my faith, what little I have will be taken from me. If the water well was flowing fresh clean water, the thought to give it away freely would be of no question. Instead, we pay a high price at the pulpit, and get little in return. There is little to go around, so we fight over what we have.

If you use antidepressants, it means you are depressed, use them to get undepressed. What is causing the depression?

The news, the food you eat, social media, sexual habits, pornography, other people's depression, sickness, poor health, stress, a guilt, loneliness, attachment to your parents view of you, your parents' ideology. Mental illness do not believe that. Work on the others and see what happens

The imprinting that takes place from our parents is an obstacle to growth. We believe the parent to be superior to us because they raised us. When we see they are flawed resentments mount from the thought of being wronged, the created ego lost after innocence takes over. Even though we see them as flawed we cannot separate them from the initial imprinting as them being somehow perfect

Read the Gospel of Mary, it is Mary of Magdala, that is a woman's truth about god.

Mary of Magdala attained gnosis, that is why Jesus held her is such high regard. Peter and Andrew had not, ignorance is proved right in its actions.

I believe in Mary

I want to know this person

To the ordinary being, others often require tolerance. To the highly evolved being, there is no such thing as tolerance, because there is no such thing as other. She has given up all ideas of individuality and extended her goodwill without prejudice in every direction. Never hating, never resisting, never contesting, she is simply always learning and being.

Translators who have not understood the woman's struggles should not elaborate on what a woman should be or not, idealism without the reality of the struggle is a lie. But the acknowledgment, is a grand gesture to her.

He has withheld from her rights which are given to the most ignorant and degraded men—both natives and foreigners.

This is pornography, prostitution, strip clubs, brothels, and the like, reduced to an object with no value, no worth, other than face value.

Prostitution has been 100% about the man the woman gained nothing.

The language of the demons, they attack the inner person.

Porn runs through the airways

Women have been pushed around for a millennium by god, men and each other. When does that end?

The Popes are the old perverts on the block, kick the old pervert off the block and reclaim your power before heaven.

The 2017 event the awakening was about a woman, who knew the 4 1/2 years later it would be pointing at THE DECLARATION OF SENTIMENTS AND RESOLUTIONS. Something a long time ago was started, I guess it's not finished. This also was a long lead coming from the Gospel of Mary, who knew?

"I have worked 40 years to make the [women's suffrage] platform broad enough for atheists and agnostics to stand upon, and now, if need be, I will fight the next 40 years to keep it Catholic enough to permit the straightest Orthodox religionist to speak or pray and count her beads upon." Evangelicals like Frances Willard, *head of the Woman's Christian Temperance Union, had gained influence in the suffrage movement, and many disavowed Stanton's religious radicalism.*

There was the misunderstanding of it roots, with Susan and Elizabeth thinking about them, let's not forget there is always support that comes from underneath, it is through the support of others, that equality is reached. This is how the spirit talks.

He has usurped the prerogative of Jehovah himself, claiming it as his right to assign for her a sphere of action, when that belongs to her conscience and to her God.

Look at the condition of the planet and humanity. Men have owned women; women are just now coming out from under the rule of men. Do not be in doubt of this fact. It still lingers in our religions that have proved themselves detrimental to our survival. Men and women are one whole, one is not greater than the other. Men have been lied to as well. It is an oppression that sits on us all.

it is the right of those who suffer from it to refuse allegiance to it, and to insist upon the institution of a new government

that woman kind are more disposed to suffer, while evils are sufferable, than to right themselves by abolishing the forms to which they are accustomed,

When Mary said this, she turned their hearts to the good, and they began to discuss the words of the savior.

You can touch the soul of another, but the touch does not remain.

The dead are not dead

Lucretia Mott

The ego discriminates against beauty, do not give your pearls to the pigs

The problem lies in the spiritual, to be pointed out as insufficient this long-standing lie. Accused of being unworthy of heaven.

The oppression comes from a mind conditioned by religion that oppresses those it touches.

Something a long time ago was started it is not finished

There is a lot of judgement saying what ignorance about the religious and their beliefs

"Blessed are the pure in heart, for they will see god" Yeshua

Do not worship Mary,

Mary is very significant to the progress of women, bringing her in line with other male archetypes of the same beliefs, has a subtle but potent shift in the consciousness. We are looking for root causes of our dysfunction.

Without Mary of Magdala, rightly called, The Apostle Mary, there is not a risen Christ, it was Mary's faith in Jesus that brought Jesus' back. Mary is the first and only student to break thru before the cross. Read the gnostic bible and get a whole picture of the Christian faith. The bible does not and has not, told the whole story, it is incomplete and in error of a truth. The image of Jesus on the cross is a dead man, the image is powerless leaving the Christian faith powerless, it fights over scraps, leftovers from men who have long been away from this physical world. God is within. Gospel of Mary, Gospel of Phillip, shows us very real picture, not an image. The image is the lie, this is one of them.

Peter also opposed her about all this. He asked the others about the savior, "Did he really speak to a woman secretly, without our knowledge, and not openly? Are we to turn and all listen to her? Did he prefer her to us? Then Mary wept

The rift between Mary and Peter that is an open wound, a resentment left open that was never resolved. The teaching of forgiveness that is taught, the energy of forgiveness is not present. Therefore, the teachings lack true understanding, the words do not equal truth. This creates doubt because, what we are being taught is not what we are feeling. Mary was completely rejected, slammed for expressing spiritual truth. The pain of that day did not just vanish into nothing, a deep rift was created. Forced to feel something that is not present.

As I made the proclamation, I went into meditation, the message was Mary of Magdala, has come for the women of the world. Believe in each other. There was an error that was never corrected, this is the correction.

The correction is in the energy field, it is a conscious shift that was never done until now. The proclamation came after the shift, after I believed Mary. This part of the story was covered up for a reason this gives women power, they become equals, that is the whole point. Jesus came for humanity, not men, but humanity. The women were still left out. I believe Mary. The bible and its beliefs about women are in error of gods truth.

I was practicing yoga on Sunday, and I felt trust, the need for and the desire to give trust. I left with that feeling in my heart I have never felt that sort of trust coming from a woman. There was always guilt or accusation standing in the way.

What is taking place with me, I am drawn back into a reality, in what was taking place. I am connecting to a real event. The energy translates, because it is real. The human mind is blind. The Gospel of Mary describes this transaction, *"That is why the good came to be with you, to enter into the essence of each nature and to restore it to its root."*

The description of the 3rd power ignorance and it being

overthrown. Very synchronistic, I did not fully understand this until this morning, I did not read the Gospel thoroughly, and put this together. Everything has been a buildup. The belief in humanity, the error of the bible, the equality of women, before heaven. Change is coming have no doubt, whether it is a swift overthrow of the dark power that rules this world, or slow evolution out, that remains beyond my understanding. Change is coming. God's word is love, there is no doctrine attached to this word, but this word rules overall. That is the change that is coming, the question is, do you believe?

Returning to the root. My feeling with Mary, eliminate the image of the curse of Eve. It's just a belief and it's just beliefs that keep us held down. Nothing more. We are controlled by what we think

This is a new state of mind, this is very recent, the Mary revelations, Believe in humanity, the image, it was an unfolding, seeds that were being planted. Sprouting when I was ready, this goes for everyone I am not unique, maybe just further along.

At lunch today I was reading, The Naassene Sermon, it was talking about the soul. It said *"They inquire not from scripture, but from mystical doctrines"*. Out of that came the Mary revelation, talking about women being the rejected stone. That led to twitter, I have been on that for a couple of days now. The corner stone phrase popped into the mind, without recognition, only to be remembered after the realization. Its these subtle seeds that are planted, then when I am ready, they sprout. Who is planting the seeds? Right? On the bigger scheme, this is how heaven talks to us. When we allow ourselves to be empty vessels, saying my life is forfeit. The attention becomes here and now, at the same time very engaged into the world, the two are one.

The language with Mary, that is gnosis. It has authority, because is speaking truth. There is a seeing and not seeing, for some it is a long process out for others, its instant. Just because you are out doesn't mean you stop growing, they are one in the same.

There was joy after all this took place, if this message was not true, there would be no joy.

Just now in meditation something came through and said Mary chose to stay behind, until the return. She sacrificed heaven for a little longer for the sake of humanity, in the earthy spirit realm. It a confusing story, but you feel it down to the soul, that something is taken place, if I could remove this person and let the world see without interference, there is no question. This is not about me, but about us. Humanity and god, some deep divine love, trying to reach us through the mire.

Luke10:42 Mary has chosen what it is better and it will not be taken away from her

How else does this come to be? These beliefs, who is in charge of your beliefs, who? Are you? Or is there someone else in charge of your beliefs?

Jesus knew the other side; he was not awake at one point in his life. He knew what it looked like, to the general population. He understood the feelings, the ridicule, the emotional pain, that was in the air, that has never left.

I was reading about Hermes today, it's funny how this stuff comes through, even on the way home. I don't want to be a god. Just denying those thoughts. It's not superior. gods are not superior to us.

The corona virus is obvious, but those that work in health care suffer more or just as much. So, who is taking our happiness and health which is ultimately our money those are our taxpayer dollars we are getting raked over the coals. This will bankrupt the Unites States. The system is broken has been for along time the virus has made it blatantly clear, that we are not in control of us.

Who are these men that we give so much power too, where did they get their authority? To disregard the wellbeing of humanity Who does that, let them speak up.

The male has for the most part had no real consideration for its female counter part. Women have had to struggle to get a voice. Out of balance.

I bought 2 "Breath" books James Nester, for some ladies wearing masks, I don't know how well they will be received, that is how you fight against the bullshit. It is not about showing the world how great you are, it is about loving another human, just because they are human. A lot of times you don't feel that you push into it. You see the error, you can longer live in the error, so you set out to change it. There is no retreating to a cave. Subtle seeds that are planted and hopefully they sprout. I gave those books to those ladies, they are wearing masks the next day, whom I to expect such radical change, when I did not, at first, second or third, glimpse

Those ladies are still wearing masks

The gods show up and science says look at our great inventions, we have discovered what it means to be human, then the gods weep over the ignorance of their creation.

Chapter 6

ABESS YIN AND THE BUDDHA

Self-worth is everything

Being taught ritual, understanding where it came from, Abess Yin. Abess Yin, showed up as an imperfect statue of something that I lacked. A girl sitting lotus on a pillow, hands at heart center. A gift once given discarded for a flee a market profit, a sharpie to cover up the blemish of an otherwise perfect being. And the lessons begin, meditation please, sit with me. meditation please, sit with me, meditation please, sit with me. Do I have to? Do as I do. That is a nice stool, can I sit on it, oh look a perfect fit. A promotion, a stool fit for a goddess. At times there is this resounding joy that comes from the heart because you understand that heaven is speaking to you, and then there are times, there is dread, because your refuse to obey heavens voice, believing your own wisdom is better than what came first. Are the lessons for me or Abess, I am not the poor statue from the flea market needing a home, who created the poor perception me or Abess? The lessons continue, we know, as if Abess was part of the crowd, who made the judgement me or Abess? The lessons continue, a shift and Abess comes to the front, welcome, who welcomed who? A table with one chair, sit and eat with me, please, thank you. The lessons continue, please don't smoke, I enjoy it, communion with the gods. Please don't smoke, I enjoy it communion with the gods, please don't smoke, I enjoy it communion with the gods. A gong replies this is not about you, the stomach moves to the throat, a correction from the gods, all is well. The lesson continues, coffee please, no thanks, we need peace. A rice cooker arrives, who came first, Abess or the rice cooker? Rice is now a staple; a palette replies that is so good! Thankyou. Come join me, thank you. A shift and the girl sitting lotus on a pillow, hands at heart center comes front and center in alignment with the stars. An identity revealed, but the identity matters not. Alas, I understand, the ritual of the heart, is the ritual of the gods. And the lessons continue

Yasodhara is Abess Yin the Buddha's wife; the world is being called out of darkness.

That is what enlightenment does it lights the way for those in darkness,
I want to know this person
The mind body connection, if I cannot silence the mind, then I will not hear the body
External inputs are felt then heard

We need peace to become present in the heart of the people
The Dolphin

When they set in motion the first beginning of speech, giving names, their most pure and perfectly guarded secret was revealed through love.

I will not be tested, by a world that lies to itself, when agitation arises this statement produces peace.

Out of sight out of mind, the destruction of the oceans
The Dolphin

Impairment of the mind was never the problem; it was the reality before the impairment.

There is no enlightenment in India
The Buddha

The greatness of Jesus, a true king, the greatest of all.
The Buddha

The Dalai Lama never became a buddha. So, if he never became a buddha then what he teaches is not from the Buddha it is from the Dalia Lama, not the Buddha
The Buddha's wife, Yasodhara
The Buddha never lost his faith
Abess Yin

India only holds a memory of enlightenment
Abess Yin and The Buddha

Take my spirit and go be woman.

Yin and Yang, Yang is the expressive, yin is the silent, and vice versa

He was an expert at ritual but had no faith. He believed in the ritual itself and didn't combine it with faith. Believing that ritual was the answer, not what ritual builds and that is faith. More ritual does not mean more faith, it just means more ritual.

Yeshua said, I have thrown fire upon the world, and look, I am watching till it blazes.

the Buddha

Chapter 7
YESHUA

Self-worth is everything

Take my spirit and go be woman.

This was preceded by a well of emotion, that pressed out of my heart, thousands of years under unjust rule, know man, but know not woman.

Whatever laws binding you to religious inequality you are released.

Jesus said, "You believe because I told you I saw you under the fig tree. You will see greater things than that."

Yeshua is a real representation of god in human clothing. He lived and felt as we feel and understood what it meant to be human.

I want to know this person

I believe in Yeshua

When Mary said this, she turned their hearts to the good, and they began to discuss the words of the savior.

Yeshua said, Whoever blasphemes against the father will be forgiven, and whoever blasphemes against the son will be forgiven, but whoever blasphemes against the holy spirit will not be forgiven

Letting go of Jesus and finding Yeshua. The Buddha

My personal commentary from information gathered, is that Jesus came to seek and what was lost, in finding one, he heals the other.

There is only ego when there is no truth. The man's ego to own women is a stance of possession. So, if I attempt to set something free, does it mean I have come to possess.

Spiritual fraud that is the makeup of our world. From Benny Hinn to Osho a long line of spiritual imposters. What we had yesterday we have today. Spiritual gurus who deplored women but still saw it fit to have sex with something they did not respect. They showed us a gate, but then did not let us pass either out of ignorance, knowing or not knowing. When the truth is seen for what it is, no longer is it difficult to spot the imposter. So religious crazy becomes a benefit to seeing the true from the false.

Yeshua is not of human decent, male and female are of no value. What is gender in heaven?

Earth is a place of astonishing beauty; it is this Eden hell where none can see that they are in hell. Blind in both seeing and hearing.

Yeshua said, If your leaders tell you, "Look, the kingdom is in heaven," then the birds of heaven will precede you. If they say to you, "It's in the sea," then the fish will precede you. But the kingdom is inside you and it is outside you. When you know yourselves, then you will be known, and you will understand that you are children of the living father. But if you do not know yourselves, then you dwell in poverty and you are poverty.

Our top gurus who sell themselves as enlightened, you represent the demons, they speak of in the Age of Kali Yuga. To be in the midst of incredible suffering, selling yourself, not what you teach.

The Chicken

Translators of religious text, translate word and form, but not power

The complexity of the weather, science has dubbed it down to a few simple weather patterns.

The Chicken

Science does not see life, therefor cannot understand life, it kills to study.

I saw one time Vladimir Putin in a picture with one of his buddies holding and looking at bricks of gold as if they could keep the gold for something more than monetary value, worthless in the life to come.

The Chicken has done more for humanity than humanity has done for the chicken.

The Chicken

Take my spirit and go be woman

Bikram, the darkness of his mind, impure, for a woman you are assaulted at first look, judged and thrown in the trash. You are beneath him; he believes himself to be superior to you, you practice his religion he is your god. Yoga was not and is not his peddle stool.

Yoga transformed the lives of those it touched, not Bikram. You did it. The yoga he gave us was a lie, only meant to bring him wealth and power, he did not sell his yoga for the wellbeing of others.

His students said, When will you appear to us and when shall we see you? Yeshua said, When you strip naked without being ashamed and take your clothes and put them under your feet like small children and trample them, then you will see the child of the living one and you will not be afraid.

Pure being

Yeshua, drank Soma

The pressing of Soma

These billionaires, just an incredible amount of money, wealth beyond measure for one man. What more can you get with another dollar?

A solution for a slum, move in with your vast wealth and change the neighborhood or country, inspiring your peers to do the same, why continue to steal from the poor by pushing the blame to the government for change.

They said to him, Tell us who you are so that we may believe in you. He said to them, You examine the face of heaven and earth, but you have not come to know the one who is in your presence, and you do not know how to examine this moment.

Yeshua said, If your leaders tell you, "Look, the kingdom is in heaven," then the birds of heaven will precede you. If they say to you, "It's in the sea," then the fish will precede you. But the kingdom is inside you and it is outside you. When you know yourselves, then you will be known, and you will understand that you are children of the living father. But if you do not know yourselves, then you dwell in poverty and you are poverty.

The Jesus I did not know, the Yeshua, I discovered.

Marcus

Just as Moses lead his people out of Egypt, so we lead our own people out of darkness into the promised land. He separated his own and made them a whole people.

The name matters not, it is what is in the heart.

The bible and what it teaches is a curse upon this world, has its fruit proved otherwise?

If I had not tasted the darkness, I would have not known the difference.

If you never believe in your own experience and your belief in yourself is based on the belief people have in you, you remain powerless. Fighting over scraps of people's thoughts about you. The right deity pushes you out of the realm of other people thoughts about you. The wrong deity puts you in conflict with other people's thoughts, about you. One gives power and the other takes.

A woman should learn in quietness and full submission. I do not permit a woman to teach or to assume authority over a man she must be quiet. For Adam was formed first, then Eve. And Adam was not the one deceived; it was the woman who was deceived and became a sinner. But women will be saved through childbearing if they continue in faith, love and holiness with propriety.

Paul had this tremendous ego, he had great pride in his religious beliefs, no different than the rest of us, when we come to believe something as truth. There was great animosity Israel was an oppressed people. So, for Paul, he saw himself superior, this risen god has come for Israel and the rest of world was benefit of this because of Israel. The bible is bias to Paul's view of things, then this view was adopted by a state authority, calling the bible divinity. Loss of spiritual freedom. Paul saw women as something inferior to what he was. That bias is sealed in that text. The bible speaks of divine things, but it is certainly not absolute divinity. This is a cheap shot, at a woman's ministry. Religion is competitive, the bible seems to skate this fact. There is a church on every corner, what do you think that there were not competing ideas back then. But because its old and dated, it has the image of being infallible and carries a weight that is not true to its statement.

It matters not what the man says, what does the woman say?

Do not believe in what Paul teaches, believe in what Jesus teaches and believe in what Mary teaches from the Gospel of Mary. Believe in Mary and believe in Yeshua, Jesus is the same but not from the bible's standpoint, Paul never met Yeshua, therefor he never met Jesus, so how did he assume the authority of Jesus?

Spiritual text is our main source to connect to source, if our written text is tainted, then our connection to source will be tainted. These old doctrines we love so dearly, are the source of our problems. Mein Kumpf is written with same the ideology as the bible. The doctrines have an energy that says, "believe me I am the truth", so the truth leads to a discrimination, in varying degrees, but the under lying theme is that there is a male deity, that is above, and we are not to question this authority. It is the ruling energy over humanity. For example, the bible says 1 Corinthians 13 says love does not discriminate, and yet it is blatant on its pages. The image of love is tainted, because it is a hypocritical source assuming it was written by god, human imperfection claiming perfection, because it speaks of god. This infallible image, one example of psychic energy, everything is the mind, control the mind, control the world. The media has a real problem. This is our change if we desire real change. The image of covid, is it real, of course, I had it. We are masking and vaccinating our children for greed, taking what is pure and putting them under the thumb of oppression, fear, cast in the name of being secure.

I know the righteousness the comes from the bible, it falls short. If a man believes he is to pass through the gate, still believing that women are not his equal, weeping and gnashing teeth, when that man is stopped from entering. If you wish to discriminate, then you will be discriminated against. I stand in testimony against the bible and its failure to bring peace to this planet.

The first line of the Christian ideology he died for you. You killed Jesus with your sin. The totem of the Christian faith is violent description of dead man of a cross. No wonder it has not had the power to heal this planet. A rejected Gospel of a woman showing us the way to peace. The most printed book ever that rejects the opinion of a woman, and we call this salvation

The bible is preached, from pulpit, ministers an attempt to display conviction will use aggressive body and over tones, so the bibles energy is cast into its hearers. No matter how it is preached it is still a man's bible that oppressed women and nature for millennia. Whatever the excuse is, it is still the bible, loaded with error, division and human injustice, in the name of God.

What is the man's bible? Idolizing destruction and pain, calling it progress for the humankind claiming superiority, as if it was a great accomplishment to annihilate the defenseless. It is great wisdom to be in conflict with another, to desire the possession of the neighbor and lust for the green grass somewhere else, instead of watering and taking care of your grass. Believing that war will create peace, instead of peace creating peace.

The abortion argument, life. Why kill life inside another life? Does the bird kill the egg before it is hatched? If it did the bird would not exist, religion does not value life, especially the mothers, they are second and cursed from the bibles point of view. So what difference does it make if the woman suffers the guilt of killing her own child. No matter how it came to be.

This is a reclamation of your virginity, before heaven.

Mocking a female deity is grounds for divorce

If you look at the oppression that has come towards women, look no farther then religion. The fear created by this heavy-handed male master coming in the form of "GOD" If the lie is exposed for what it is why do we tolerate its existence? It is oppression nothing less.

In the parable of the lost sheep, the soul is the lost sheep, that Jesus goes to find. The repentance is church doctrine.

There has not been one book that has been more destructive to humanity than the bible.

For the biblical scholar who promotes the bible as infallible divinity, how can it be called perfect when it pages create and promote discrimination. Why do you still apologize for its defect?

Science is blind.

From the Buddha

Three things cannot be long hidden: the sun, the moon, and the truth.

The mind is everything. What you think you become.

You only lose what you cling to.

Peace comes from within. Do not seek it without.

Do not dwell in the past, do not dream of the future, concentrate the mind on the present moment. The present moment without a god, is limited to the present moment. Falling short of god realization

Health is the greatest gift, contentment the greatest wealth, faithfulness the best relationship.

It is a man's own mind, not his enemy or foe, that lures him to evil ways.

We are what we think. All that we are arises with our thoughts. With our thoughts, we make the world.

You, yourself, as much as anybody in the entire universe, deserve your love and affection.

No one saves us but ourselves. No one can and no one may. We ourselves must walk the path, the gods show up when needed.

When the unenlightened mind tries to describe things only understood by the spirit it reduces the spirit to the mental sphere of the conditioned dichotomous mind.

There is always duality, yin and yang but not separation only harmony.

The Buddha

Chapter 8

THE UNIVERSAL WAY CHINESE DOCTRINE

Self-worth is everything
Horses' Hooves

H orses have hooves so that their feet can grip on frost and snow, and hair so that they can withstand the wind and cold. They eat grass and drink water, they buck and gallop, for this is the innate nature of horses. Even if they had great towers and magnificent halls, they would not be interested in them. However, when Po Lo came on the scene, he said, 'I know how to train horses.' He branded them, cut their hair and their hooves, put halters on their heads, bridled them, hobbled them and shut them up in stables. Out of ten horses at least two or three die. Then he makes them hungry and thirsty, gallops them, races them, parades them, runs them together. He keeps before them the fear of the bit and ropes, behind them the fear of the whip and crop. Now more than half the horses are dead. The potter said, 'I know how to use clay, how to mould it into rounds like the compass and into squares as though I had used a T-square.' The carpenter said, 'I know how to use wood: to make it bend, I use the template; to make it straight, I use the plumb line.' However, is it really the innate nature of clay and wood to be moulded by compass and T-square, template and plumb line? It is true, nevertheless, that generation after generation has said, 'Po Lo is good at controlling horses, and indeed the potter and carpenter are good with clay and wood.' And the same nonsense is spouted by those who rule the world. I think that someone who truly knows how to rule the world would not be like this. The people have a true nature, they weave their cloth, they farm to produce food. This is their basic Virtue. They are all one in this, not separated, and it is from Heaven. Thus, in an age of perfect Virtue the people walk slowly and solemnly. They see straight and true. In times such as these the mountains have neither paths nor tunnels, on the lakes there are neither boats nor bridges; all life lives with its own kind, living close together. The birds and beasts multiply in their flocks and herds, the grass and trees grow tall. It is true that at such a time the birds and beasts can be led around without ropes, and birds' nests can be seen with ease. In this time of perfect Virtue, people live side by side with the birds and beasts, sharing the world in common with all life. No one knows of distinctions such as nobles and the peasantry! Totally without wisdom but with virtue which does not disappear; totally without desire they are known as truly simple. If people are truly simple, they can follow their true nature. Then the perfect sage comes, going on about benevolence, straining for self-righteousness, and suddenly everyone begins to have doubts. They start to fuss over the music, cutting and trimming the rituals, and thus the whole world is disturbed. If the pure essence had not been so cut about, how could they have otherwise ended up with sacrificial bowls? If the raw jade was not broken apart, how could the symbols of power be made? If the Tao and Te – Way and Virtue – had not been ignored, how could benevolence and righteousness have been preferred? If innate nature had not been left behind, how could rituals and music have been invented? If the five colours had not been confused, how could patterns and designs have occurred? If the five notes had not been confused, how could they have been supplanted by the six tones? The abuse of the true elements to make artefacts was the crime of the craftsman. The abuse of the Tao and Te – Way and Virtue – to make benevolence and righteousness, this was the error of the sage. Horses, when they live wild, eat grass and drink water; when they are content, they entwine their necks and rub each other. When angry, they turn their backs on each other and kick out. This is what horses know. But if harnessed together and lined up under constraints, they know to look sideways and to arch their necks, to career around and try to spit out the bit and rid themselves of the reins. The knowledge thus gained by the horse, and its wicked behaviour, is in fact the fault of Po Lo. At the time of Ho Hsu, people stayed where they were, not knowing anything else; they walked but did not know where they were going; filled themselves with food and were happy slapping their bellies to show their contentment. This was what the people had. Then came the sage. He brought the cringing and grovelling of the rituals and music and infected all under Heaven with his offer of benevolence and righteousness, which he said would comfort the hearts of all. As a result the people desired and longed for knowledge, and warred against *each other to gain the advantage. Nothing could stop them. All this was the fault of the sage.*

The Universal Way is undiscriminating virtue, there is no way you get there without belief. It is an open route guided by the universe to those willing to answer its call.

The Great and Original Teacher

Thirty years it has been 30 years in the pursuit of god, the yearning, the finding, the losing and once again finding. There is nothing more my heart desired most, my heart desired peace.

Believe in each other, Believe in nature that is the one true god.

THE UNIVERSAL WAY

The Universal Way is the destination of all spiritual efforts of humankind. It serves all people's lives, everywhere and always. The Universal Way conveys the deep truth of all conscious elaborations of the human mind. It contains the vast and profound essence of the human spirit. Thus it transcends all religious teachings, leaving them behind, like the clothing of a bygone season. The Universal Way is the goal of all sciences, but is not locked at the level of the intellect. It cuts through all wasteful skepticism and inexhaustible searching. Thus it surpasses all sciences, leaving them behind like historical relics of the past. The Subtle Essence that is sought by all sciences and all religions transcends all attempts to reach it by means of thought, belief or experiment. The Universal Way leads directly to it and guides you to reach it yourself by uniting with the Integral Nature of the Universe. The Universal Way is like the master key to all doors leading to the inner room of ultimate truth. It is the master teaching of all teachings, yet it relies on no religions and no experiments. There is no need for intellectual or emotional detours that cannot serve the lives of all people everywhere and always. Follow the Universal Way beyond all boundaries to the heart and essence of natural life itself

The gurus don't confront the evil of the world, they say its there, and pull you away from it, but don't confront, men of equal status. Gurus have followings in the millions collectively just as much as world religions. Leaders of spiritual country, if they came together united in one cause what impact would that have on our planet. Claim that spiritual power to change our existence, so it comes from the spirit and not from a bottle.

If peace is preached, then why is there fear.
It is peace that we are looking for, it is fear that stands in the way.

The old religions of yoga, the chasing of a pose. Forgetting who is doing the pose seeking possession of perfection that will never be reached, both mind and body. Keep the yoga its universal, lose the religion, the image of the form being most important

The Gospel of Mary has been around for more than 100 years, it is not preached or understood from the pulpit. Because it teaches religious freedom and equality. This is what Jesus taught. Who better to trust his wisdom then to leave it with a woman.

Our religions are at war with one another so how can they bring us peace? Its leaders certainly won't take off the costume, for world peace, that is asking a little too much of their gods.
Believe in one another

Chapter 9

THE LOTUS LOFT

Self-worth is everything

The bird sitting on top of a cage is symbolic of freedom Feathers that build faith.

Couple of months ago I was in yoga class, and I was thinking about what to put in the offering shell, I will put seeds in the shell for the birds, an offering to the birds. I walk out of yoga and in the parking lot is a large feather.

Yoga practice, yesterday I saw the amassing of birds around where I live. Through a lot of experience with unexplained synchronicities, there is no doubt nature speaks. This is where my faith comes from. I then gave my yoga intention to the birds; I asked the earth for their wellbeing. Yoga practice began with a slow flapping of wings. Then the whole practice became about nature. The poses took meaning the energy was focused. Sunbird dips, Sun salutation, "salute the sun" the wrapping the of arms humbly bowing and giving my energy to the elephants, warrior 3 with wings with honor. The mass of birds were crows, a butterfly with a thought of how I love the pigeon pose. I come home and dragonflies abound and see and hear the fluttering of a dove. Yoga just took on a deeper meaning, a deeper connection to all that is around me, what a blessing that nature speaks in these ways.

Garumaju lyrics

Creating concrete visions of a macroscopic prism With a brilliant optimism and appropriate ambition To be open from the center, redirected to the moment This is it love, this is it love, unrestrainable nature

We can change it from the edges, we can challenge all our borders There is always a new leader, there is always a new order Our pathway is proceeding and the way is always changing We are free from what prevents us to realize our destination

Oh...

Free from all old stories I've been told I walk through the valley of my own shadow Free from all old stories I've been told I walk through the valley of my own shadow

Awareness is my virtue, and I'm grateful for the search to Dive deep within my own mind and to trust the intuition Of the lives I've lived before this, our essential form of gnosis It's a simple form of freedom; it's as smooth as inhalation

Oh the exhale is releasing all the tension I've been feeling On the surface and beneath me, I'm connecting to my spirit And I'm here now right before you; I am present in this moment And my life's work is to honor the great beauty all around you

Oh...

Free from all old stories I've been told I walk through the valley of my own shadow Free from all old stories I've been told I walk through the valley of my own shadow

Creating concrete visions of a macrocosmic prism With a brilliant optimism and appropriate ambition To be open from the center, redirected to the moment This is it love, this is it love, unrestrainable nature

This is it love, this is it love, this is it love, this is it love

No one ever comes to yoga thinking I just need to lose some weight

The best version of my self

Truly Truly

The best pen ever

Best day ever

There are times when explosions of gratitude come bursting from my heart, thanking everything in my world for being in my life. "Thank you for being in my home"

Thank you, it bursts out in gratitude, spontaneously.

The spirit brought yoga to the west, not some guru.

The embryo in the womb of the mother, then, he is born. Reflections on a sound bath. The sun is the Golden Embryo, a goddess

In the beginning the Golden Embryo arose. Once she was born, she was the one lord of creation. she held in place the earth and this sky Who is the god whom we should worship with the oblation?

Wake up with one mind, my friends, and kindle the fire, you many who share the same nest. I call Dadhikrā and Agni and the goddess Dawn, all joined with Indra, to help you.

In a vision I see the being throw the spear, at yoga thunder rolls through.

Teaching yoga or something the requires a following, is tough personally, every time we go to teach, our happiness or self-worth is tested by the opinions and feelings of another. That is why teaching service is a tremendous vehicle for spiritual growth or disillusionment success and failure two sides to the same coin.

Yoga has music that is not always agreeable to the conditioned mind, in class I became agitated, and wanted to blame, I put my mind into another and allowed her to enjoy the music she likes.

Yoga this week has been memorable, the depth of class from high to low, I used to believe that harshness was the way to learn, I touched the subtle path the error was corrected.

Look at all the birds

Spiritual practice produces take a way's,

This is preached doctrine, which is no doctrine, just felt being.

The greed of men causes our pain.

The soul is without label and compassion is without label, we shy away from the things we need. Who, what, where, why, when and how?

Yeshua is a badass, one the most profound spiritual teachers known to man, this thought popped into mind yesterday in class and again leaving class tonight. It brought up the story of Yeshua raising Eleazar from the dead, Mary and Martha's younger brother, a friend to Yeshua. A story thrown into myth, made real considering the deep emotional ties to Yeshua. *"When Yeshua saw her weeping"*, *"he raged at his own spirit, harrowed himself"*, *"Yeshua wept"*, *"Yeshua again raged inwardly and went to the tomb" "in a great voice he cried out, "Eleazar, come out!"* This is the man who Mary followed and believed; her testimony can be nothing but truth.

Then Mary stood up, greeted them all, and said to her brothers, "Do not weep and do not grieve or be irresolute, for his grace will be fully with you and will protect you. Rather, let us praise his greatness. He prepared us and made us truly human." When Mary said this, she turned their hearts to the good, and they began to discuss the words of the savior.

Yoga stoned but not stoned, oppression does not create confidence, Yeshua believed in Mary

Oppression does not create that kind of confidence, belief creates that kind of confidence, equality and understanding of the feminine soul, which is both male and female. If Yeshua had the views of Paul or Peter, Mary would have not never stood up. The shame thrown at the physical female is a spiritual blindness, if the woman led the man astray, then it is the woman who leads, it has always been that way.

The power of the bowls, I was wondering why those that have the bowls, the bowl, the gong, the mantra, why not have sound group bath, the sole practitioner and inspiring practice in others. Sound vibration moves the mind. You don't have to know the anatomy to make noise, but its affects are just as far reaching

"Look at this window: it is nothing but a hole in the wall, but because of it the whole room is full of light. So when the faculties are empty, the heart is full of light. Being full of light it becomes an influence by which others are secretly transformed."

The Lotus flower totem

The light in me honors the light in you.

Rigidity of posture was it the final goal?

Learning to teach yoga, the ability to lead someone through a practice. I benefit off the routine of others.

Yoga has always been about the gods, not science.

Yoga is a created practice that has not reached its fulfillment, knowledge of posture is not the end result, the spirit has not run its leg of the race.

Yoga stoned

A Ganesha mudra, the elephant shadow, the synchronicity of life and the intelligence all around us showing us to trust what supports not what kills. Saturday, a gourd found in a parking lot that said take me home, then seeing the shadow, but there was no preconceived idea of what was going to show up, it was absent from the mind. A tribute to the elephants of the world

There is a lot of ego attached to awakenings, we never get past the awakening. We slip right back into darkness. The guru has not got passed the awakening. They don't teach the holy way.

ECKHART TOLLE

present moment

Truth

PRESENT MOMENT

eckhart tolle

Don't get lost in the present moment

The spirit has no knowledge to hang over your head. In our world today knowledge is power, but it has not led to virtue. True knowledge leads to a virtuous life not in lip service, but in the heart. So, when I say that knowledge of posture is not the end result, it is not a ding of knowledge of posture just a shift in perception. That is all that it ever is, perception, for me and for you. I don't know your perception, I only know mine, maybe. My perception says if I don't practice what I preach then my knowledge is false. If I acquire 1 million followers, because of my great knowledge of posture, but the heart has remained dark, then what good is my knowledge of posture. It is the spirit I seek thru posture, not more knowledge. Yoga is a universal religion, when practiced without the desire to gain power through knowledge of posture, leads me to the gate. Don't let the knowledge of someone else prevent you from going through the gate. It is your gate. There is the tree of life and tree of knowledge, one leads to the spirit, one leads to more knowledge. There is always the fork in the road, but the pursuit of knowledge, is more knowledge, the pursuit of life, is the spirit, the spirit is life. Just a shift in perception. Pursuit of knowledge needs an audience to exclaim its greatness, pursuit of the spirit, forces you to let go of the opinions of others.

Yoga in its genius allows the practitioner to check out, long holds, after exhaustive flows, the movement of energy. That is why it appealed so much, it allows time for reflection on otherwise unseen thoughts and emotions, dating back, seconds to decades. If my search in yoga is the attainment of perfect posture, or trying to forget my day, I have missed the point of yoga. There is no criticism coming from this observation of personal growth, without yoga structure, posture and breath, the latter is not possible. The discovery of base yoga movement and breath healed my long-standing injuries that long exhaustive flows could not, teaching final posture for fame is not yoga.

Trust that was the intention, and the dolphins, three other things One universal mind, life

If I bite the hand that feeds me, I am wrong, I am fed spiritually through yoga practice, and those sanctuaries. Sanctuaries change but the feeding continues, flowing with gratitude.

I love yoga and believe in yoga. I love the teachers, their studios and what they believe in. They believe in a higher way of life. There are other forms of moving meditation but this one is the one I ascribe to.

When you follow a guru, you never exceed their found state of awakening.

The fight has been ongoing for millennia, it just changes costumes.

Think about what you think about, I have come into a different understanding of this empty mind philosophy. If you are assaulted from external inputs and then made to believe that it is coming from within, there is never any chance at breaking through, you will always be the problem. The criticisms of yesterday

An empty mind sees the thinking mind. If I am thinking in yoga, and I can't think of anything, I guess my mind is empty. There is always this push to empty the mind, to let go, to let go, to let go, fear can arise pulling us back from the letting go. The silence or the emptiness of mind. I guess my disagreement with the current yoga philosophy on the male side, it did not see the oppression of women and did not stand up, because it did not see or did not understand. So, how empty is your mind.

We live in this world of complete bullshit; people say one thing but think and feel another. There is no truth between mind and body. The body is felt emotions, and the mind does not understand the body.

The conflict in our world comes from the top not the bottom, the bottom is always suffering, because the top has the power.

The nipple, I was playing the gongs, a breast feeding, the breast of life. How do you discriminate against the mother?

Working it out on the mat. What better place to deal with your emotions, then in silent movement of the body.

Teaching yoga is a complete service, you no longer teach for the pose but for spiritual attainment, nothing has changed except awareness

The breath is a confusing topic, from experience it does not translate, moments touched then lost. Write something down and take into practice, See what comes up. The breath has on countless occasions placed my mind into a higher realm of thinking. The breath is superior to the thinking mind, when the mind is challenged by this thought, it will disagree, because the breath is not attached to the ego.

The romantic idea of love, for most of us, there is that one or two we fall in love with, then after that it is a chasing of an emotional imprint that can never be reprinted. That is why porn is popular with men, because romantic love is about sex.

The mind throws daggers of energy in pleasure and pain. It is through these daggers that we shape our world around, either for building up or tearing down. Racism, inequality, hate, all conditions of the mind. The daggers are thrown in judgment of others trying to defend the daggers that come against us, an unseen war that shapes are relationships and existence. Who is it that throws these daggers?

Demons attack the soul, never letting it rest. Finishing mediation, sitting back to enjoy the moment, wanting to feel the spiritual presence. Loud angry footsteps from the neighbors, their fear entangling with my peace. My thought goes back to the lotus loft comment, the demons attack through my energy not allowing my peace to entangle with lotus loft. That is how demons work, we all connected. Even the demons.

The rulers of the air accuse us night and day thru each other.

Practice and teaching are two different paths that reflect one another. Without the practice the teaching becomes just empty words. Yoga is a spiritual practice

The imprinting process, spiritual imprinting is like first love, second love, they bite and find joy, then they wear off, the second time you understand what it is. So, you hold on to it, but unless you work at keeping the love fresh, it loses its luster. When we come into contact with those that are still in love, the energy speaks for itself. There is no right or wrong, it is just a different frequency, one is higher than the other.

What more can I say about yoga, is their gurus that bought this religion are flawed like the rest of us, the hypocrisy in our minds is the same that is in their minds, they have not transcended anything more than you. Yoga practice is for you. Even dating back to the Patanjali without the struggle of the hypocritical mind there is no understanding of another. If the music played was of my liking, there would be not temptation of resentment, sound, just as much as sight.

It is in this understanding of those we think, that are different from us, brings equality

I come to yoga this morning two birds on the roof, one with wings open showing me where the feather came from. This is life that is all around us.

When we were children, we dreamt of being in the clouds, they had a magic appeal that sent pure mind into heaven, we grew old, and the clouds died, the clouds are a god within themselves.

Yoga studios are sanctuaries for spiritual growth, the energy is always living and active. just like the word of god.

The sutras, virtue, control and letting go

mind, body, spirit

It will always come back to you and be about you. Problems arise because someone else wants to make it about them. This is ongoing for me the letting go of someone else. Trusting in the letting go.

The drama of the mind is always there, on and off the mat, this ongoing conflict with our own doubt.

Transformations happen over periods of time, spiritual transformations can happen in an instant

BELIEVE

Chapter 10

RELIGIOUS CRAZY

Self-worth is everything

Waking up, November 2017 I didn't quite comprehend what was behind it, the image. I could not see, then suddenly, I could see, but couldn't comprehend what I was seeing. There was an evolution that needed to take place, I had to rid the body of this left-over energy. It is quite difficult; it is a painful process. A deep level of acceptance, allowing the ego no excuse, sometimes you win and then others you don't, but there is this ongoing push forward. Belief, that is the fuel for the engine. With the belief you learn to push into the pain, instead of the pain pushing in on you. Your effort is to become superior to the pain. There is no other way to think, there is no wrong. You are waiting to be put in check, testing the boundaries, and something is pushing you. You know it is from the divine.

These words they might be identical to other people's experience and maybe I am the one that doesn't see it. No, I see it.

It is a lie; I don't know how you guys either cannot see it or you don't want to.

There is so much disbelief thrown our way, you can't see that. It is confusion on top of confusion, this energy being pulled around in many directions. There is a miss, the gurus are like gods, that is what is taking place. The gods love human worship. That has been the feeling, I don't know, what is about take place, I can assure you that something is. But there is a return, that is happening. These beings don't lie. Love does not hurt, lies cause pain. These beings are pure light. We are not in control; we are not at the steering wheel. There is a darkness that sits over us. How and why, I don't know. I just see it, that is enough. It's like the drug addict who is lying to his family about his problem, his life is spinning out of control everyone sees it except him. He thinks he is in control, that is denial. We are human.

The gurus are meant to oversee our evolution, if their egos stand in the way, who is to blame? If they need the credit, what's that say about them? If our leaders oppress those they lead, what does that say about them? Why do you need to oppress? Who said that is a better way?

There is this vague idea of how to pursue god, light, love and sound, but as much as a guru says it's there, you never quite feel or understand what he says he has. Never quite understanding and feeling, his description of what he says he has. The image created by spiritual experience, then embellished upon, gibberish. They never can get past the love and light, and get into the darkness within all of us, and uncover what keeps us from understanding the love and light we cannot find. We must dig through the darkness, to taste a piece of the peace, then work to maintain the light within, always being consumed by darkness without.

Once you have the initial breakthrough in seeing the mind, meditation becomes understandable, never really gets easy. Also, when it becomes a devotion to the gods, it becomes necessary ritual for becoming your best self. Devotion brings strength and conviction; you understand how hard it is to remain in your best self. The clear conscious is the unblocked path to the higher mind where the gods dwell. My diet, vegan diet, I don't consider myself vegan, no label needed, because I abstain from certain foods. When the bar is set high with no ceiling, the whole planet raises its frequency. Meditation is first and foremost to practice, what blocks meditation practices, meditate and discover. A temple rises around you with no idea it was coming. Athena is real and her government below. The guru needs the label of guru, that is the problem with guru, they deem themselves special, the true being sees the guru in everyone, and believes it the true being has discovered the guru within and doesn't need the label of guru. I preach salvation of the soul; I believe in the soul and its salvation before heaven. Purpose with authority, it is god inspired teachings, salvation is judged by the conscious, your conscious, not in defense of the religious scripture, but conscious before the soul and before god. It is a woman's movement,

Porn is this gross magnet of insecurity, it touches the soul
The Nymphs

I deepened my meditation practice from July of 2017 to present, meditation accompanied with virtue is the key that opens the door, all else are impostors. There is no enlightenment without virtue, virtue is enlightenment, seeing the one universal life in all things. Seeing and understanding the creative mind.

I am helping people just as the universe has helped me to overcome. My virtuous commitment to humanity has been best represented in the fulfillment of my dreams.

Text for reading

The Unknown Teachings of Lao Tzu.

The gospel of Mary

The gospel of Thomas

Gnostic Bible

The sayings of the Buddha reflections for every day, William Wray

The Hua Hu Ching, complete works of Lao Tzu, Hua Ching Ni

The Odyssey, by Homer

The Rig Veda

The Woman's Bible, Cady, her commentary packs the punch, she is the scripture, not the scripture

The Way of Chuang Tzu, Thomas Merton

The Book of Chuang Tzu

As a man thinketh, James Allen

The Yoga Sutras

The Bhagavad Gita

and the like

If you read for knowledge of the spirit, you will find what you are looking for. Reading is partial practice. There are many authors who take a lot of credit for what they write and do not give enough credit to the spirit, it is the spirit that has brought us here, not your ego.

Always remain focused on the deity, Religious crazy

"*The greatest fear in the world is the opinion of others, and the moment you are unafraid of the crowd, you are no longer a sheep, you become a lion. A great roar arises in your heart, the roar of freedom.*"

At one time this guy was something special, a bottom feeder that fed on ignorance for his own benefit, the spirit, not the ego, did the work.

And Paul still defends his ministry

Eckhart gets stuck on himself. Or people get stuck on what Eckhart says he has. You never lose the reality of other people.

You get in and then get out, you don't continue trying to get back in.

Abusing mind altering substance goes nowhere, without mind altering substance, rigidity goes nowhere

The gods live through us, they enjoy the subtle sense pleasures of the body, but not abuse. The demons abuse the body through the senses.

Sincerity is a prerequisite to finding faith

An Email to Harvard scholar Karen King there was quite few more of the same message, over a few months.

*I removed God authority from the Pope, what more do you need? Preach the gospel, equality before god is the gospel. Everything fixes itself balance is restored. This is how it happens, one inspired beyond doubt, a history of events, then the coming out. Our religions are dead, detrimental to our survival, a deity shows up, we question the belief, it just a change in the godhead. The masculine to the feminine, the feminine becomes dominate thought, the masculine becomes inferior, still needed for balance, but not war. **www.breakingfree71.com** The website is a collection of experience and history of my awakening it is old thought new thought, but not preached. I have little doubt will be pillaged, for profit, the best sellers meeting a contract commitment.*

The goddess who presides in human affairs

The one who understands Heaven and understands the ways of humanity has perfection.

There are many times when I feel the judgment of the mind

96

looking at the external being and the conditioning of this world. It says religion is false, you are a fraud. Where would this energy come from it was not created by religion itself. Are highest forms of altruisms is marred is gross darkness, when one steps away from this darkness and calls it for what it is, it questioned and doubted, the mind rarely sees any truth.

The Gongs and totems have been a real treat, Abess Yin, the Buddha, Best Day Ever, Seeds from the sunflower, Mary, The 3 suns and their two relatives. The Birds and their freedom, they are for the most part a free being. Nature represents freedom, wild animals are free beings. The frog quilt, the elephants and the tree of life. A dharma wheel that is turned, a symbol of change, a star without meaning, a neckless for a goddess, feathers to fuel the fire. Sparrows on the wall expressing confidence, a dream catcher I didn't know could catch. Pinecones and a duck and I cannot forget the captain's wheel and a hand to help it steer. Taking correction from the spirits listening and not listening the constant chaos coming from the gods on the wall. Never knowing what is coming next, being completely surprised at its arrival but always filled with joy. New discoveries underneath the candles, the gifts of gratitude that overflow with words that say, I love you. Ancient Greek literature without commentary and comprehension. A gnostic take and the discovery of another Jesus. A question mark in the sky and still I ask why? Birthday of a god with a son in mind. What can I say and what more am I supposed to do? Edits to a story forgetting a family that I once lost but is now on the mend. Blue suns and new challenges and the lyrics of songs pointing the way. In a crowd not of my gender, trying to understand my gender. So, again I say what more I am supposed to do? The appearance of the white pigeon with a message in mind. So, I say again what more I am supposed to do? The cawing of crows and the singing songbirds giving and gaining trust, that I do not feel worthy to have. But why not me and why not world peace, what prevents us to realize our destination. The cannabis connection judged as an imposter, from the skeptic that has no solution. The cannabis reply follows, do you ever just go, to each other's houses play gongs, use cannabis or not and talk about god. Fresh flowers and lit candles Gongs that talk and joyful noises. Demons understood the angels are not. Totems have tremendous power; they carry in them the energy of life. It is belief that we are looking for.

There is thought of an ego, of being spiritually aware.

If I take the ring of power for myself then I am no longer spiritually aware, the ring of power belongs to women. Belief is confidence, the ego destroys beauty then claims it was not. There is no inequality ever!! You cannot hide the oppression and say that never it existed, or things have been made right, that is a lie. Men have not changed their ways and religion has not repented of its sin. Like I said religious crazy. But religious crazy is not blind. Belief brings the manifestation of courage; it is belief that sets the soul free.

Because you cannot see I am here to please. So, why do you grope and tease. Insults and criticisms at a loveliness so fare. You raped my lands and have devoured my worth, covering me with clothing that only conforms to your eye. Centuries gone without a single reply why must I fight for this right? When do you change, when do recognize your great insult upon a country that is not rightfully yours? Who is this that speaks? I don't know I say, I am this man taking a stand, I guess? What more I am supposed to do? Religious crazy

Rights and wrongs There is never hurt feeling over matters. There can't be you don't go back we all need correction. It is the way it works, see the wrong, feel the wrong, let go of the wrong, and continue to push forward. all ways letting go of the wrong. With no judgment of the wrong, but always having to let go of the judgment of the wrong.

And just yesterday, I looked into the clouds, and said that looks like an hourglass

Who is higher on the food chain ants or humans?

Some say technology is better than a natural plain life, if you desire your every movement to be watched and questioned then technology is for you. Religious crazy is a natural plain life

Chew on this for a few years

FIFTEEN The master continued, "Kind prince, tolerance is a necessary virtue in everyone's daily life, but for a universal integral being there is nothing that needs to be tolerated or labeled as tolerance. Tolerance exists only in the relative sphere. Lao Tzu Hua Hu Ching

Because there is no tolerance. Not what you think it is. It is fuck you, don't push in on my rights Lao Tzu preached and lived inner power. He still preaches and the word he preaches is living and active.

Their thirst for power and blood.

We are given intelligence of the physical world to improve the quality of life for the myriad of creatures, the hoarding of intelligence for profit and power is the same, as money for profit and power. We are given intelligence to understand the physical world, not to dissect and destroy. Not in a billion years will the human with its current perspective, ever match or succeed in understanding the physical world. The human will die of ignorance because of its thirst for blood and power A disgusting display of greed and incompetence.

You think the Dalai Lama does not view himself on You Tube, or his many documentaries. Any that post stuff, you go back look at it. You think he does not do that, he teaches nonattachment, he is pretty attached, you can't be. Therein lies the problem, it becomes powerless, it only gets you so far. He just a religious old man, with a title that has no power for change, in a world that desperately needs power for change.

You must bypass the image to get there, the image does not represent what you are looking for.

You have two older African American women walking every morning sticks in hand, the neighborhood. The purest of the purest energy doing something to better themselves, and they are being lied to, and they are hurting themselves with the masks. That is a blatant crime against humanity.

The real power has their own global network their transactions, go undetected they move around in secrecy way above any laws that govern the rest. Impossible for the world to have any success of ever surviving. They view themselves as something more than they really are, remove their created image, there is nothing there. Oprah is a lady, a black lady with no power. Tell the world your secrets, and where has your power gone? Oprah commands a massive audience of women believers, she is a believer. Women are believers, hence their vulnerability to deceit, innocence not weakness. Is this speculation or conspiracy, why would it not be true, everything is the image, there is no truth. Santa Clause enough said. They learned that it was image, create an image it sells, and it defends. But they didn't know how or why they were creating the image, the image itself sold success, your image is everything. Even though it stepped on everyone and everything to get there, there is no guilt, the image is success. Eckhart Tolle is a hypocrite, he says the same thing, but gives it to the ego, at the sametime creating an image for himself, spiritual blindness. The awakening for all of us, is that if he did it, he who pointed it out, but became it, thrusts all of us into blindness about the nature of our world. The top guru never went after the bible, in fear of the crazy's, are they anymore lost than the religious crazy's they were afraid to confront. Again, it shows the blindness of the guru and their lack of felt awareness to the suffering all around us. Instead, they give copy writ quotes, selling themselves as superstars of morality, and that is this just it, selling themselves. Nothing changes, because there is no substance to the created image, very little is felt experience. They are selling an image of themselves, not what they teach, both the teaching and the image lack substance. Splashing around in puddles of water hoping somehow to get drink of water. Might be a little harsh, but look what our children have access to, my parents were not responsible parents. Their quotes are about living in the present moment is bliss, the current present moment is ugly, the male child with a cell phone, his present moment is porn, 2 or 3 times a day. Since I am here, religious crazy.

You know life is just super painful, it hurts, it does, there is no denying that. Happiness is bullshit, how can anyone be happy during so much pain? We cover it up with some image created by an illusion of how we think other people think of us. Always trying to keep up the front, that is how fear is created that defending of the lie, causes the pain. Yet, through the pain, through the lie, we come out victorious on the other side. I am telling you there is another side. It still hurts but there is no more image to defend, that is the beginning of real freedom.

Disbelief that is what comes back.

If I am truly an enlighten being we are talking a major shift in our conscious evolution. I believe it to be possible. If I can't win those around me or at least make some sort of difference there is no way to win the world. It starts with what's in front of your face. You win and you lose, but what else is there? Nothing seems to compare to that commitment to humanity. This internal change you are changing for those around you, you eat your ego, you stop the mind argument. Its win and lose, but the progression never stops. Just complex layers in between.

There are some hard feelings that it might not work out, you still give it an effort, it doesn't matter win or lose. It is just a state of progression toward some happiness There has to be a deep underlying peace that goes with it. That is the reward. If it was not better, why push for it? The peace comes and goes, but "life becomes helpful". I remember that from the Eckhart Tolle days, that is one of those sacred phases, it gets implanted into the psyche that is recalled again and again.

We have this great tolerance to suffering, we are numb. There is no way around that, one man has 100 billion dollars, and there are people within his grasp that are somehow suffering, there is no urgency to fix anything. I am not blaming anyone; I am just pointing it out. If you are human, there is no blame. That is the whole point.

The message, believe in humanity, humanity is you, but I don't know how to get there. It's the message. We are given pointers, women are authoritative equals, this deep discrimination towards women, that women must address. Women are a formidable force and should not be afraid. These rules come from inferior men or beings. That is how you should view them. They do not come from god, God, they don't come from heaven. And are not in your best interest. Oppression, how is that helpful to you? Why do the religious intuitions have the biggest discriminations? What sort of deception is taking place?

I got the flower sermon, *Mahākāśyapa*. June 2018 around there. I had already experienced the transmission phenomena, but this one helped me to understand in proper context how they take place. A definitive clearing of the subtle body, something with power has touched you and has left some knowledge with you, that quite can't be understood in words. The Lao Tzu transmission was similar, but I didn't understand it as a transmission. Nov 2017. Then there are numerous events and similar experiences that just become part of everyday life.

Old 2017 post

Attachments and gurus, Can the awakened consciousness go dormant? Going dormant by means of attachments to the external. Let's say profound insights given at one-time lead to fame and fortune these understandings also lead to unchecked ego. Because they are gifts they remain with those to whom they were given, like opening a door its stays once its opened. My question for proclaimed gurus at some point depending on the student, the guru would become a hindrance to further growth. The student must find their own way or the transformation is limited to the guru's perception of enlightenment and not the students true authentic experience with consciousness. At what point are these so-called masters selling themselves or true conscious experience? The frequency in which I am speaking I believe to be high, just in observation with my own path. What I write about is experience and my own unfolding. Does the gurus experience stop? Can you get spiritualized, for example finding Jesus, let say at 19 I have this overwhelming spiritual experience, but years later the power transform is stopped. Is there a difference? I hope you get the line of questioning. So, the guru in consciousness can be misaligned, as much as the preacher at a Christian church or any other religion. Spiritualized, so the participation with consciousness is halted because the ego has assimilated the conscious. That is my understanding of what I see and feel in the consciousness movement, the buddha at gas pump interviews are very eye opening, it's not words it the energy that speaks. The gurus are a sign post and should not be held in any regard, as superior. Lastly look and feel for yourself the motive in which we are taught, the till, the blue bag, the basket, donate to my cause, it is a sign post pointing to enlightenment with a price tag on it. The Buddha says, you can't teach enlightenment you can only point the way. I question the sign post that has a price tag. Is it really pointing the right way? Let me reiterate, all gurus are sign posts nothing more, Jesus, the Buddha, Lao Tzu and all enlighten masters are sign posts nothing more. We all have what they have and with deep conviction this should be conveyed

I am worthy

Religious Crazy

Chapter 11

THE GHOSTS

Old post early 2018

The ghosts or Non-being entities NBE's

Without a doubt ghosts exist and have influence in the physical realm, to what extent it is impossible to say, but since my coming into an extensive contact with that realm, I would say their influence is wide-ranging and difficult. The feelings associated with certain entities is not agreeable at times, they have a way of opening the subtle body and exposing the truth to the energies the mind is interpreting. I owe a very large part of my cultivation into my view of enlightenment to the ghosts or more rightly worded, non-being entities.

Non-being does not mean that something does not really exist, but that it exists beyond the senses, time and space. Supernatural beings extend their life force freely to the lives of form and no-form and at the same time keep themselves unformed and supernatural HHC 46 Lao Tzu

As this last year has unfolded my experiences with NBE's was crucial on the path of self-cultivation. As I opened my self-up and let go of long standing doubts the NBE's made their way through, going from heavy to light, and even light to heavy. Feelings associated with thoughts and physical experiences with people, places and things would reoccur like a ground hog day experience until the lesson was learned or more likely until the energy was changed or removed from my own subtle body. This letting go or change was synchronistic to things read in spiritual texts, mainly the Hua Hu Ching, and for most the part the experience came before the reading, so as to seal the experience in the subtle body. This subject goes deep into the fact we are creators, but without awareness of what we are thinking "creating" its hard to determine what effect are influence is on our present environment. Even if our life outwardly is viewed as successful, if inwardly we still feel competitive and at odds with the world, then we are still creating disharmony for ourselves and others.

It's extremely difficult to be honest, but if you look at the world, that is you and that is me, there is no separation.

As described in the Final awakening blog, the initial contact was for the most part was pleasant, I encountered and witnessed some very unusual events. Came into conscious contact with numerous NBE's to what purpose that is beyond my current understanding. I was thinking nobody just starts writing this stuff or believing a certain way, its all influenced by something. Again, that is the unknown, just reconfirms my beliefs that no one knows, so don't hold too tightly to anything cause eventually it will change.

If there was one energy that the NBE's exposed the most, was doubt. Doubt was a core belief that I held on to that also caused the most pain. In Buddhist text, doubt is considered suffering or an affliction. Doubt made me suffer, not just in the mind, it's a very painful energy, like the feeling of someone you love doesn't love you back. That is the energy it produces in the body. Then you breakdown even farther, lets say the competitive mind, "You cant do that" I don't believe you" "You're not good enough" "You're your not smart enough" and list can go on forever.

This whole awareness of doubt came clear one morning at work, after the NBE's event. There is a ghost that resides where I work and on multi occasions I would sense its presence, look up and for instant see its image. Well, I found myself doubting either the entity or myself. If I doubt the entity then everything that took place was a lie and or I doubt myself, then the pain continues. That instant I made the decision to quit doubting. But the decision was just the beginning of letting go of years of built up energies stored in my body, that were wreaking havoc on my personal life and those I am associated with. The NBE's started coming through layer after layer, very painful at times, then followed up with epiphanies into the nature of own existence. Allowing for changes in the psyche, and slowly life just began to change. For awhile life became very dark, I was living with deep paranoia of people entering my apartment, but in midst of all this my meditation practice became deep and profound, and I understood the process of what needed to take place. Peace had not arrived, and awareness was hitting peaks. Anyone familiar with kundalini transformation, this describes on it so many levels what has happened to me, but I don't like the kundalini title, though true, becomes I believe obstacle of further attainment. As I felt the pain of fear and doubt and looked with the consciousness at how the mind interprets various energies, I slowly transcended into a higher realm of realization. I can see mind energy, there is line of separation between the conscious self and ego mind. Ego is not real and only survives be giving it energy or more mind energy. I let go it lets go, easier said than done. If you seek enlightenment, what ever your view of this is, open the subtle body the let the non-being entities through, because in a few short years you will be one too. One simple statement, I am open and then watch, feel and let go.

A given epiphany from an NBE

From November 2017 to mid-December, I was without work, completely orchestrated by the universe. During that time I picked up more meditation 4 to 6 hrs. some days. Well, I am meditating and it's not going anywhere, then out of nowhere, this old figure like person walks into my 3rd eye and bumps me off this chair, there was an immediate frequency change, like I leveled up in a video game or something, and the lesson passed to me was, **"There is nothing the mind can think, that is worth holding on to"** That was my beginning into no mind and its frequency. I think to the person who sat down was Lao Tzu or the being that represents the teachings in the Hua Hu Ching. Maybe that is pretty grandiose thinking!

All these events came through the opening of the NBE's they all have their place, an archangel to a lowly demon looking for reconciliation searching for the right frequency it can transform with. Look past the thinking mind and dig deep into meditation and quit stealing from humanity and give something back to yourself.

All views are subject to change

A friend asked are not demons negative, as I was lighting up some palo santo to clear the air. I replied, maybe a lower energy but demons just point out our flaws. So if we are looking for real change don't despise what they are telling you, because ultimately its you and me they are trying teach.

Chapter 12

CHAPTER 4

2018 Sometime Old post.

A term I learned from the teachings of Eckhart Tolle, I see it now as universal truth or maybe just a byproduct of an overactive ego mind. I learned through application of what he teaches to identify and dissolve its tendencies. It is pain, no other way around it, it is an energy whether it is lodged in the body, physical or subtle or projected outward at some time or place finding its way back for renewal into fresh new pain or for transmutation into something divine once seen in the light of consciousness.

The dissolution of the pain body takes time and a lot of effort, it hurts, and I will say confidently there is no easy way to go about it. Enlightenment without direct experience on the subtle operation of the pain body and the lessening of its effects on our lives and the world, enlightenment is not possible. Awakenings are possible, waking up consciously and enlightenment are of a different change. One is like a newborn baby; the other has trained at their craft, dissolving the pain body is a process of refinement. The layers run deep perhaps back to humanities birth, from my experience we can dissolve not only our own pain bodies but of others connected to us, which is limitless.

These past 5 years has taken me into the depths of my past life in this present lifetime, from childhood to present, and I found layer after layer of self-doubt, which in turn created pain. I must admit that I do give the core of its birth to my upbringing. As of right now I do see things more of needing to learn something in this present lifetime and then I move on and with some certainty consciousness doesn't cease after physical death. This physical world is just some stage in our evolutionary process of our beings, short but important, maybe not so short considering I don't how many times I have lived to discover what I have now.

I realized that even in meditation, to meditate on peace or insight is not enough to gain a higher understanding of the universe. There is thick coating of gross heavy energy that blocks our understanding of the truth of all things. Even if we want to see we can't and even if think we see it, we still only seeing partials. The more we process the pain and let go the more we see, meaning running to the pain not away. As we release that energy our frequency changes, we just understand things, without trying or reading. Conflict subsides without having to go out of the way to make amends. This understanding brings peace, because it nullifies conflict within from those that seek power from others through their spiritual understanding. I believe to, the frequency will never be as high as it can be when having to pay for or donate to hear some else's take of spiritual matters. The motive if not completely altruistic downgrades the frequency. I read about this in The Hu Hua Ching plus that been my experience since my own frequency has changed. The world is just reflection of YOUR inner self, dig deeper commit to meditation, Upanishads, Hua Hu Ching, Yoga Sutras, study the ancients with and without commentary meditate on that energy, and light will shine through. They the ancients respond to sincerity without conflict, it takes a lot of effort, to shed layers, layers are attachments, and attachments are just thoughts.

Universal Way and the eternal truth of life depend on the development of individual self-awareness, not shallow social movements for the multitudes. What is needed is the total awakening of all, so that the majority of people will know to eliminate negative influences in their lives and do what would benefit other people. Universal cultivation is individually based because it involves personal self-transformation and breaking through the individual's cycle of insatiability. Each individual is responsible for his own evolution, but true achievement comes mostly from one's virtuous fulfillment in helping and serving his fellow human.

"Kind prince, liberation from physical bondage and high spiritual freedom are not beautiful pavilions in the air. They require a process of continual transformation and evolution with the biological aspect of a human being as its foundation. It involves breaking through the cycle of life and death. It forms the hope of every individual who would attain the freedom of life. Most people's awareness is limited to the short span

of their own lifetime and the superficial sphere of their daily life, as they stubbornly insist that these ordinary cycles are the final truth of life. They superstitiously cling to the hope that they will receive salvation through their religious beliefs, thus they see no need to learn the Universal Way of cultivation."

Lao Tzu

Chapter 13

THE CHURCH OF CHRIST

The Church
Old post 2017

The church was at onetime all that mattered much laughter, joy, and love based on a common good, save souls, save the world. The bonds of fellowship surpassed any family relationship I had ever known. I loved the fellowship and fellowship love me, and probably the closest thing to heaven that this physical plane had to offer. It was the purity of heart the genuine spirit of love that radiated throughout fellowship, that was so powerful. College days late nights at Denny's pretending to study, uncontrollable laughter sometimes at my expense and that of others, but it mattered not, love was the common denominator. Early morning devotionals, singing songs, and giving hugs, praising a God who redeemed our souls with a loving grace. Camping trips and cookouts filled with a one-pointed focus, love the lord your God with all your heart, mind, and soul and save the world. Those times truly taught me what love is at a glimpse.

Bible studies and discipleship, showing people the error of their ways, confession of sin with no ulterior motive. Campaigns to save souls as if they needed my help to be saved. The church gave me what I never learned at home and that was a belief in myself. God found me when I needed its help most, I was beat up emotionally and void of any real understanding of love. I was around the church maybe ten yrs. and I loved it; I loved the truth the bible studies the deep connections that I found in spirit. This Isaiah 55 type relationship. So, I have no ill toward the church, the church has been the truest expression of God that I have come in contact with. My friendships, the support, the truth, the earnestness to live the scripture as they were taught. The commitment to purity to live above moral standing of society, called to higher plane of existence. Really trying to intimate the standard Jesus set, but like the bible says all fall short. The ego: 2 Thessalonians 2 Is not about Satan, that is the ego metaphorically speaking not one man, but a mode of thinking, The church is not immune.

If everyone that left the church or was kicked out twice, took the standard and left the ideology the world might be saved by now. But men and their egos always must screw it up for the rest of us. I guess that is part of lesson humanity is trying to learn.

I am not excluding myself from error but the whole point of on a conscious awakening is seeing the whole picture can you see whole picture?

The whole picture says I viewed my reality from my perception, meaning every other interpretation was neither right nor wrong, from an outsider looking in I have the same view as the insider looking out at all the other perceptions. So, there is no truth, but that which is your own.

Needing to be right, just an honest look at the pattern of thought and how divisive the preemies of the one and only church is or even Christianity. How does such a violent god turn into a passivist? Almost comical, with the argument that God passed on those teachings for you, for your perception that you are right. No one else can be right, it is infallible, perfect without blemish. Does this same line of thinking not follow every, dictator, mass genocide, warped ideological view that has ever tortured our planet? Can we not consider history and not see the core error? Jesus was appalled be what he woke to, and his disciples did not understand the depth of the teachings, so the teachings got warped very quickly, within a few generations the established church was killing other humans in the name of Jesus. Now is that Jesus? A healer and a man who wept with great empathy of over the suffering of humanity, is now the vehicle of pain and grief. You can't explain away history. Does it really matter what the Hebrew says and Greek, is that knowledge not a stumbling block into seeing another truth, not born of bias.

John 13:34-35 "Love one another, as I have loved you and all men will know you are my disciples". Consider this statement, how did we come to put Jesus is such a narrow box. Can we see the use of this teaching without subjective interpretation, can you not see the truth from untruth, rules and rigid dogmas used only as a means of control, it's not even that cynical, it's just ignorance, not negative as dumb just without knowing? Again, it goes back to unconditional service to humanity, that's what the spiritual greats taught without conditions. Imagine a world, where leaders were of the deepest virtue, lowly and humble, and walked among many, refusing extremes of luxury, power and pleasure, the people understood by their example and harmony was possible with all living beings, because they themselves where in harmony with all that is. Just like the Buddha, and Lao Tzu and many enlightened masters, Jesus taught universal harmony not divisive concepts of self and others, wrong and right," A new commandment I give you love another" Then reference that back to 1Coth13. What else is there?

The bible and has some powerful truths, when used in proper application has the power to change and heal but, if used in context for control or conversion turns toxic and becomes very destructive to those it is imposed upon. 1 Corinthians 13 love is there no higher expression of life and what we are supposed to represent then real love. If we take this one chapter and made it state doctrine and no words we added or taken away it would save the world and the planet. The core error is that we take this chapter and try to use its essence as a right of claim that my religion is superior to yours. The whole chapter contradicts any bias or judgment assumed from other ideological beliefs stemming from religions. Love does not discriminate, if Jesus was the ultimate portrait of love. Then labeling of saved not saved is not love and cannot exist in Gods eyes. Yet if I removed Jesus from the equations, and take that vehicle of indiscriminate love, it heals all wounds, it cures all diseases, and it forgives all sins, nothing can stop that power. But as soon as we pin the husk of that grace and the majesty of its flight, becomes a poor reflection. Digest that chapter and see, feel and experience what love really is, without label or bias. This chapter represents the evolution of humanity not someone's interpretation of right and wrong. The power to heal or power to control and destroy.

My opinion of the church now, does it matter? It doesn't, the universe is unknowable to limit your view on something you don't understand is ignorance and ego. If you say, you know, how? From a text written by who? Who validates their character. Certainly not Christian history, judgment, condemnation, and separation and not of the universe. Jesus was right, but not the western view. Jesus embraced the lowly of low, prostitutes and tax collectors and was condemned in his day for not adhering to established beliefs. "I AM the way the truth and the life" he speaking to the I AM or the consciousness that is in all of us. Mercy, compassion and love.

Chapter 14

THE NEW
REVELATION

1. *Believe in humanity, that is you. What does that mean? Love one another.*

2. *You do not need a guru. The connection is equal. Listen and learn but not believe that they have something more than you.*

3. *There is not one hint of inequality, that exists between woman and man.*

4. *The image is a lie.*

5. *The main dilemma with the human existence, is believing in images without awareness.*

6. *God's word is love*

7. *Love is god's word*

8. *If the mother and father of the house returned and saw that their children has outgrown them, settled their disputes and loved one another, they would simply join them and become one of them, sharing in their love for one another. What more could a mother and a father ask for?*

9. *Love without knowledge is blind, knowledge without love is powerless, love with knowledge is god. God's word has unfathomable knowledge because it is love.*

10. *The power is in us, the word of god is in us, love is in us. That is our light.*

11. *Believe in humanity, separating the wheat from the weeds. If the so-called believer cannot believe for the unbeliever or even for other believers, what makes them believe they are going to heaven? They are one in the same.*

12. *Love is fire that is coming from above, the message cannot be a lie, no lie can come from love. Believe in humanity. That is the message.*

13. *The bible has some curse on it, it is not complete. Do not seek salvation thru it. Look at its fruit and know its truth*

14. *This world in its current state is false, do not believe its images without awareness of what they represent.*

15. *I have stepped over some line and there is no looking back, step over the line and don't look back.*

16. *If humanity believed in humanity, it would fix itself. It would have no choice, it believes.*

17. *Love is without doctrine, but it contains true knowledge. Belief is without doctrine; it also contains true knowledge.*
    If you desire true knowledge, then practice love and belief without doctrine.

18. *Why would we not believe in humanity? Because some image says look at me, don't at them, look at me. Know that to be the false self.*

19. *Find the whole human and feel its fire.*

20. *Let religion go and seek gnosis*

21. *"There is nothing the mind can think that is worth holding on to" This was a transmission in late 2017 from a being that represented the The Hua Hu Ching*

22. *The Hua Hu Ching, is a full version of the diamond sutra. without the labels, respectively. It teaches true knowledge.*

23. *I comment on what works for me. There are many paths to god, once you get there it becomes clear the language is the same. Learn to speak that language.*

24. *Facing the unknown has an element of fear*

25. *The leadership of this planet is low grade.*

26. *Perfection is something sold by the image. It is a lie.*

27. *The image loves the image, but that is not the same love.*

28. *These are not great people, it is atrocious, how we treat each other and how we treat the planet. It is really disgusting, it does not matter whose fault it is, just take responsibility for it.*

29. *It is in our nature to love one another.*

30. *The weather fears no one, it just rolls, feel its power.*
31. *There is no not being worthy, unworthy is a lie sold by the image.*
32. *Secrets don't exist in heaven, so make sure you unload them, so "you" can get into heaven.*
33. *Secrets are like weights attached to our souls; they drop us in frequency.*
34. *31, 32, and 33 are from Mary the contribution is relative to the number in kindle text in which this is inspired 31, 32, 33 close enough*
35. *The gnostic teachings are right, I have not experienced all of them, but the orange is an orange.*
36. *If you desire what is false, you will become false, if you desire what is true, you will become true.*
37. *The image is the beast, the beast is the image, described in the book of Revelations, destroy the image destroy the beast, the image hates humanity.*
38. *Satan is not understood and accused being of a false image.*
39. *I don't understand everything I say, I guess that makes me human. As for Satan female not male, generous not selfish.*
40. *Our sons and daughters have their own path the choice is theirs.*
41. *Eckart Tolle has his place, the pain body revelation. He didn't take it far enough, who is the pain body?*
42. *We are ruled by what we worship, 3 billboards in sync, money, sex and sickness, we are ruled by what we worship.*
43. *Love has no doctrine, if my beliefs in god separate me from love, then I automatically renounce that god, and return to gods word which is love.*
44. *It is in the rebellion that we find freedom from the oppression.*
45. *The physical is the spiritual*

46. *The white man has never known racial inferiority.*
47. *I have seen a light, not in me but in us, you are the light I speak of.*
48. *Life is meant to be happy, not some gloomy hell of mental torture, produced by external pressures.*
49. *Those that take power from others live in a state of constant fear, fearing that someone might take their power.*
50. *Those that take power have no power to give, so don't give them your power.*
51. *Free yourself from fear and the need to take power from others will, goes away.*
52. *It is only those that create the pain, that cannot see those that receive the pain.*
53. *Paul's version of what Jesus is and what he represents failed this world.*

Conclusion

AN ODD TALE TO ITHACA

10

yrs. gone I stand in a field in a broken boat looking out on an unkept pasture, thinking I am Ulysses somehow on the last leg of some voyage, how and why I am here parallel universes intersecting as time goes forward but the stories remain the same. We find god in the new age, and we write new scripture

Athena throws her javelin, Mary in stride on the wings of heaven

Athena showed up and said drink some wine. Not my will but your will be done. We trust in Athena, Abess Yin

The divine poets have always been with us heard but not understood, music, literature, art, scripture and cause.

The Monarch flies a graceful dance of caring purpose.

Led into the grove a fairy tale scene of dragon flies and magical vegetation a secret spot a lone bromeliad, come and see it says, dig for the treasure, a grass land fairy's spell blocking the way.

The Arachne weaves now in plain sight, before just a spider's web.

At the beginning

How does one come to endure such agony in life? To never be at rest within or without, fighting for a cause that only leads to death. The soul cry's out please father take this away, 3 times a plea and 3 times an answer. Still the agony returns year after year, the unrelenting pressure brought about by family, friend, and foe alike.

At last, I discover the demons what I run from are my demons, to hold me check to keep me from believing, believe in anything but don't believe in yourself.

Athena poured a heavenly grace upon him.

Sex is the farthest thing from our mind.

The Nymphs

we love you.

At the end

I stroll into a beach at sunset thinking, has this been here the whole time the moon shows itself lighting the way and feathers from the birds.

The Odyssey, by Homer

That is right Marcus, Athena heard our prayers, Susan

THE HOLY SPIRIT

We write new doctrine; Self-worth is everything
What do we believe in? Who is our god? Touched by the holy
spirit
I saw the white pigeon today
That is the final decree
The holy spirit
The holy spirit, I am life.

THE YOGA PRACTICE WITH NOTES

From the gods, gentle yoga. A sunflower flow. Deep breathing and movement

Top of mat hands to heart center, set your intention.

We count, we breath, we remember, when we remember we praise. Salute the sun and bow gently to the earth, the Mother Goddess.

Songs, This practice is for me. Say it loud one time, Say your song for this practice

Deep nasal breathing unless noted in flow. The focus is counting, breathing, movement, praise.

Practice begins: 10 breaths

Starting position: Standing top of the mat hands at heart center.

Movement: Inhale through nose, exhale through the mouth (1) to 5 Inhale, exhale through nose. (6) to 10

1. 20 half bends, **Song, this practice is for me**

Starting position: Hands at heart center, feet hip width distance
Movement: Inhale hands up over head palms to touch look at hands exhale fold hands separate to shoulder width, fold ¼ 0r ½ head hangs heavy shoulders are relaxed momentary pause at the bottom of the breath and inhale hands to touch look at hands. (One) repeat to 20, last one hang for 10 breaths shoulders swings freely. Inhale hands to touch, exhale hands at heart center. (20)

2. 10 forward folds legs substantial bend in the knees. **Song, this practice is for me**

Starting position: Hands at heart center, feet hip width distance

Movement: Inhale hands up over head palms to touch look at hands exhale fold hands separate, to shoulder width, fold head hangs heavy bend in the knees hands tented fingers to rest on mat shoulders are relaxed, one full inhale stomach to chest and exhale, inhale up arm overhead palms to touch exhale hands to heart center (One) repeat to 10, last one for 5 breaths. Inhale hands to touch, exhale hands at heart center. (10)

3. 20 cat cows. **Song, this practice is for me**

Starting position: On hands and knees, hands in line with shoulders and knee in line with hips
Movement: Inhale arch the spine drop the belly, tailbone tilted up exhale round the spine pelvis to chest and look at the pelvis push through push the hands to round the spine (1) Repeat to 20

4. 10 Sitting hip to heels, arms overhead. **Song, this practice is for me**

Starting position: Sit back heels to hips, hands at heart center
Movement: Inhale arms up over head palms to touch, look at hands and exhale hands down by side, head hangs heavy. (1) Repeat to 10 hands to heart center

5. 10 standing on knees, arms overhead, breath is reversed. **Song, this practice is for me**

Starting position: Standing on knees, hands at heart center, exhale and inhale have switched.
Movement: Exhale arms up over head palms to touch, look at hands and exhale hands down by side, head hangs heavy. (1) Repeat to 10 hands to heart center

6. 20 breaths sitting on heels. **Song, this practice is for me**

Starting position: sitting hips to heels, hands at heart center. Movement: Breathe Inhale and exhale (1) Repeat to 20

7. 10 Seated twists. **Song, this practice is for me**

Starting position: Hips to heels sit back on heals, hands to heart center

Movement: Inhale fill the lungs, exhale twist to the right, look over your shoulder, inhale to center hands to knees, exhale to the left, look over the shoulder, inhale to center fill the lungs (1) Repeat to 10, last one hands to heart center.

8. 10 Standing on knees side bends **Song, this practice is for me**

Starting position: standing on knees hands at heart center

Movement: Inhale palms to touch, exhale bend to the right, right arm to side, look over left bicep, inhale up palms to touch, exhale bend to the left, arm to the side, look over right bicep, inhale palms to touch (1) repeat to 10 last one hands to heart center.

9. 10 Standing side bends, breath is reversed. **Song, this practice is for me**

Starting position: standing feet shoulder width apart hands to heart center.

Movement: inhale then exhale up palms to touch, inhale bend to the left, left arm down to side, look at left foot. Exhale up, palms to touch, inhale bend to the right, right arm down to side, look at right foot, exhale palms to touch (1) repeat to 10, hands to heart center.

10. Seated folds. **Song, this practice is for me**

Starting position: Sit up legs out in front toes toward the face legs engaged hands down by side palms flat slight push from palms for body lifted

Movement: Inhale hands over head at shoulder width exhale half bend palms on the mat, inhale reset to starting position. One full breath (1) repeat to 10 hands at heart center.

11. 10 Cross legged twist **Song, this practice is for me**

Starting position: easy seat right in front of left hands at heart center

Movement: Inhale twist to the left, body lifted, look toward you left shoulder, tented fingers touch the mat, inhale to center hands on knees, exhale twist to the right, body lifted, inhale to center, hands on knees (1) repeat to 10 hands at heart center.

12. 20 Breathing rest **Song, this practice is for me**

Starting position: laying flat on you back hands down by your side.

Movement: easy breath

Part Two
Song: **This practice benefits me**

1. 20 half sit ups **Song: This practice benefits me**

Starting position: laying on back arms over head, legs engaged toes straight up.

Movement: Inhale, then exhale up all the way out, inhale arms over head to starting position (1) repeat to 20 last one hold for 5 breaths

2. Seated folds. **Song, this practice benefits me**

Starting position: Sit up legs out in front, toes pointed out, legs engaged hands down by side palms flat on mat.

Movement: Inhale hands over head at shoulder width exhale half bend palms on the mat, inhale up flow. One full breath (1) repeat to 10 hands at heart center.

3. 10 Seated twists. **Song, this practice benefits me.**

Starting position: Sit up legs out in front, toes pointed out, legs engaged hands at heart center

Movement: exhale twist to the right, look over the right shoulder fingers tinted on mat, inhale to center hands on thighs, exhale twist to the left, inhale back to center hands on thighs (1) repeat to 10 last on hands to heart center.

4. 10 Seated folds legs substantial bend in the knees. **Song, this practice benefits me.**

Starting position: Sit up legs out in front, toes pointed out, legs engaged hands down by side palms flat on mat.

Movement: Inhale hands over head at shoulder width exhale half bend palms on the mat, inhale up flow. One full breath (1) repeat to 10 hands at heart center.

5. 10 wind removing flow. **Song, this practice benefits me**

Starting position: Lay on back, hands overhead
Movement: Inhale, exhale bend the right knee pull it into the arm pit, inhale down arms over head, Exhale repeat on the left (1) repeat to 10

6. 10 supine twist flow. **Song, this practice benefits me**

Starting position: laying on back, arms out to a tee, legs bent, soles of the feet on the mat
Movement: Exhale, bent legs fall to the right, look to the left, inhale center, legs and head, exhale legs fall to the left head to the right, inhale to center (1) Repeat to 10

7. 10 straight leg lifts. **Song, this practice benefits me**

Starting position: laying on back arms up overhead.
Movement: Inhale, exhale left leg comes straight up toes pointing towards face, inhale down, Exhale, right leg comes up toes pointing towards the face, inhale down (1) Repeat to 10

8. 10 straight leg and arm lifts. **Song, this practice benefits me**

Starting position: laying on back arms up overhead. Back of head remains on mat
Movement: Inhale, exhale left leg comes straight up toes pointing towards face left arm up simultaneously, inhale down, Exhale, right leg comes up toes pointing towards the face right arm up simultaneously, inhale down (1) Repeat to 10

9. 20 bridge lifts **Song, this practice benefits me**

Starting position: laying on knee bent soles of the feet on mat arms down by sides
Movement: inhale bring lift the pelvis, to bridge and hold exhale down
(1) Repeat to 20

10. 10 crossed leg neck rotations. **Song, this practice benefits me**

Starting position: Hands at heart center, head straight, inhale, exhale look to the left, inhale look center, exhale look right, inhale look center, exhale look down, inhale look center, exhale look up, inhale look center. (1) Repeat to 5 then switch legs 6 to 10

11. breathing rest

Starting position: laying on back, arms down by side
Movement: Easy breath

Notes from practice, modify, adjust and create for your own practice. Be gentle with yourself and the body responds. There are many forms of moving meditation all of them are beneficial to us.

1. Breathing last 20 arms circle counterclockwise for 10 up then clockwise down to half or full inhale up
2. Last 5 the bottom, cow the body head tilts up
3. Transition
4. One full breath at the bottom
5. 5 breaths at the bottom head are heavy
6.
7. At the end fold forward walk the fingers out one breath at a time and then up one up one breath at a time until all the way the up
8. Steeple the fingers on inhale up, let go on exhale The arm that this at the side, pull or extend the shoulder down
9. Steeple the fingers on inhale up, let go on exhale Same on the shoulder, neck rotations on last one, inhale, exhale, right, ect... same on 8
10. Toes pointing up, exhale toes pointing out
11. Breathing rest star

Part 2

1. Work the sit up all the way up to full forward fold. Grab feet, 5 breaths at the bottom head rotation inhale up exhale down Modify by bringing legs to chest
2.
3. Opposite shoulder extends down the leg, neck rotations last one right left down up
4. Grab the feet by the arches press the foot forward.
5. Arm pit is a big place move around. Look right and left.
6. Palms are down, move your hands up past the shoulders

7.

8.

9.

10.

Part 3,4,5,6>>>>>

ABOUT THE AUTHOR

I have not tasted success; my life is but a failure if it was not for the gods. When I cry out the gods respond, how come no one cries out, so the gods can hear your cry. At this time in my life, my life is in complete control of the gods. I quit my job at the new year, I have no income, I am living off credit cards and some silver I had stashed away. My car payment was past due, it would not let me sleep, I refused to pay rent, because they wanted me to sign away my soul. I wait for the eviction to come; my argument is just. My chest is tight, and it is hard to get up, I meditate 2 hours a day, drink wine, smoke pot, and do a lot of yoga. I email those I think have influence trying to get my point across, fanatically, why tweet just email your take.

Life is dreadful at times a pain in the body, waiting for doom to come, but doom is not in the head, just a pain in the body. Then life is filled with joy letting you know you are not alone. Let me teach you how to cook. Try this yoga. Meditate. Sit outside prayer hands at forehead and the acknowledge the sun a greater being than you, the moon, the earth. Go camping, go camping again. Write your book. Write our book. The heart screams out let me be closer to this being.

Printed in the United States
by Baker & Taylor Publisher Services